MIDNIGHT MOVIE MONOGRAPHS

TWIN PEAKS
FIRE WALK WITH ME

MAURA MCHUGH

Midnight Movie Monographs

TWIN PEAKS: FIRE WALK WITH ME

Copyright © Maura McHugh 2017

Cover Art and Design
Copyright © Neil Snowdon 2017

Series Editor
Neil Snowdon

Published in June 2017 by Electric Dreamhouse, an imprint of
PS Publishing Ltd. by arrangement with the author. All rights reserved by the
author. The right of Maura McHugh to be identified as Author of this
Work has been asserted by her in accordance with the Copyright,
Designs and Patents Act 1988.

First Edition

ISBN
978-1-786361-20-2

Design & Layout by Michael Smith
Printed and bound in England by T.J. International

PS Publishing
Grosvenor House
1 New Road
Hornsea, HU18 1PG
England

e-mail: editor@pspublishing.co.uk
Internet: www.pspublishing.co.uk

Contents

1 . . . . Prologue

7 . . . . David Lynch

19 . . . . Twin Peaks

31 . . . . Fire Walk With Me

112 . . . . *Selected Bibliography*

'Through the dark of future's past'

Prologue

THE TEMPTATION WHEN EXAMINING *Twin Peaks: Fire Walk With Me* (FWWM thereafter) is to become bogged down in the minutiae of its originating TV series, and lost in the labyrinthine theories which have sprung up across multiple online forums and discussion groups. *Twin Peaks* is one of the first true Cult TV shows that thrived upon fan interest in the nascent Internet era, and colonised space on the World Wide Web from an early stage. Despite comprising only 30 episodes, the world of *Twin Peaks* has endured and fascinated its adherents long after the show was cancelled.

While *FWWM* is hugely indebted to the TV series *Twin Peaks*, the film exists as a separate artefact and possesses its own unique identity. It functions as a prequel to the series, but ultimately it is a hymn to Laura Palmer, the fetishised mystery girl of the original series, who was only glimpsed in death through a kaleidoscope of epistolary details: diaries, video tapes, and second-hand recollections.

In *FWWM* writer/director David Lynch brought his attention wholly upon Laura and her struggles in a direct and unsettling fashion. The film deals with spiritual crisis, incest, and the suffocating realities of small town America in a way that *Twin Peaks* couldn't represent. *Twin Peaks* was a co-creation between Mark Frost and David Lynch, but *FWWM* was always Lynch's vision (though he shares the writing credits with Robert Engels). In *FWWM* the town is seen through the prism of Laura's experiences, so its spectrum of darkness is more visible. The film, which was rated R by

1

the MPAA due to scenes of sex and violence, was also not limited by the bounds of television content restrictions, and did not shy from showing the awful realities of Laura's predicament.

At its best cinema is about producing unforgettable moments that sweep the audience up with their grandeur or immense introspection. TV is often obsessed with the small moments of many lives. Thus *Twin Peaks* is about *the town and the community* but *FWWM* is all about *the person*.

This difference in focus is why *FWWM* was always going to be a hard sell when it was released in 1992. Gone were most of the quirky scenes about Tibet, coffee, and pie beloved by fans of the TV show. The charismatic, slightly kooky, FBI agent Dale Cooper and the 'Scooby gang' of off-beat investigators (both official and unofficial) were side-lined in favour of shining the spotlight firmly on the source of their obsessions: Laura Palmer, Homecoming Queen and cocaine addict.

The dead object of the TV series became the live subject of the film, and it's not coincidental that there was a significant blacklash against *FWWM* from both critics and fans. Laura was liked better as a dead girl wrapped in plastic, than as a seductive, erratic teenager teetering on the edge of mental instability. Her impending death is a troubling prescience that looms over the film, and it's a credit to the luminous and engaging performance by Sheryl Lee that her radiance offsets the gathering dark and gives the audience hope despite the inevitable tragedy.

Cinema is a demanding medium, and it requires a ruthlessness by the editor and director in cutting out swathes of material to refine the message and select the defining scenes. For *FWWM* it was an even bigger challenge since the film was also trying to pay tribute to a TV series with a wide array of characters and storylines that comprised over twenty-three hours of material. According to film editor Mary Sweeney the first assembly of *FWWM* footage was five and a half hours long.[1] When Lynch and Sweeney fire-walked with the film through its many editing sessions they forged it into its unique form, and so it has remained. Lynch's interest is offering mystery to the audience, and he does so by embracing oddness and moments that seem out of place and time.

---

[1] John Thorne, *The Essential Wrapped in Plastic: Pathways to Twin Peaks* (John Thorne, 2016).

Though he had the opportunity to craft a 'director's cut' of *FWWM*, Lynch has determinedly stuck with the version he originally released. He's satisfied with his strange, difficult film, and that's the version that will be the primary focus of this monograph. Most of the 'missing pieces' of the film were made available for the Blu-ray boxed set edition of *Twin Peaks* and *FWWM* released in 2014[2], but they remain separate to the film. They are the discarded chips on the floor after the sculpture is revealed, serving to placate obsessive fans and, in some cases, tantalise them further. But, while they may be useful, there is a reason they are not part of the final film.

There are other elements to consider, including the original script and older versions of it—but again, they are not the completed vision. At best they are indicators of the process of refinement that Lynch and Engels embarked upon.

The process, while interesting, is not the final product. Once a director takes a script and embarks upon the process of manifesting it changes are inevitable. Sometimes they are deliberate, but often they are spontaneous and due to the alchemy of actors, environment, crew, and shooting schedules. Above all Lynch is an instinctive director who reacts and adapts as his creation unfurls. Lynch's aesthetic is that of his first vocation as a painter. His brush is the camera, the paint is the characters, and the canvas is the scenarios and sets. He understands that the very act of concreting the idea changes its form, and on occasion it might escape one's control.

But he is not averse to that either. His aim is not to make tidy sense of things, because we do not experience the world as a straightforward narrative. Rather he wants to allow the story to reveal itself in an oblique way, encouraging the audience to immerse themselves in his world. The puzzle hooks you in, but it is the peculiarity that captivates you. At the core of his scenes of unreality lurks a resonating truth. There is a tantalising illusion that you could understand everything if you could just figure out one key phrase or strange incident... this acts as a lure to allow the story permission to engage with your critical sense, while the images and sound sidestep it to access a more primal circuitry. It is also the reason why Lynch's work is so often deeply alarming to watch.

---

[2] *Twin Peaks - The Entire Mystery, And the Missing Pieces* (CBS Blu-ray, 2014).

Lynch's experience as a painter trained him to finish a work, hang it, and allow observers to come to their relationship with the art without having to guide them. He has said:

Painters don't have to talk. Every idea was in another language, down, deep inside. I never had to bring it to the surface. So things were pure and, you know, better than way. I didn't have to justify anything. I could let it just come out. And that's why talking about things isn't a totally satisfactory thing.[3]

Lynch the filmmaker makes extensive use of visuals and audio to cue the narrative, developing into themes and codes that occur repeatedly in his work. It is his default means of communication. Symbols, icons, flickering lights, distorted sound, musical leitmotifs, song, and a distinct colour palate generate the atmosphere. He has a knack for spotting unlikely actors who can inhabit his abstracted notions and bring his characters fully to life. He allows the actors leeway and trusts them to delve deep as he guides them. Most of his actors speak of him respectfully, and they can achieve illuminating and moving performances under his direction.

Lynch has continually resisted explaining his work. He understands if you pierce the mystery with knowledge then it deflates to a narrow understanding.

You start articulating a certain thing, and then you suddenly see it for what it is and the magic goes away a little bit. It's tricky. When you talk about things—unless you are a poet—a big thing becomes smaller.[4]

Language in *FWWM* does little of the heavy lifting when it comes to explanation, if anything it is to be mistrusted and subverted. At times it is nonsense, or played backwards. It's often poetic or idiosyncratic. Martha P. Nochimson, in her analysis of Lynch's films—*The Passion of David Lynch*—notes that Lynch's first wife Peggy Reavey "told me that he has always been intensely wary of how we are 'dictated to by language and

---

[3] Chris Rodley, (ed.), *Lynch on Lynch* (London: Faber & Faber, 2005), p. 40.

[4] Ibid., p. 27.

things like language."'[5] Chris Rodley also quotes Reavey on this subject. She claims that Lynch was almost "pre-verbal" when she first knew him. "He didn't talk the way a lot of artists do. He would make noises, open his arms wide and make a sound like the wind."[6] This frustration with language appears early in his work, such as in his short films *The Alphabet* (1968) and *The Grandmother* (1970).

In this book I will indicate the themes that thread through some of David Lynch's films prior to FWWM, and also touch upon the original TV series to offer context, but my primary interest is to explore and open up *Twin Peaks: Fire Walk With Me* as a powerful account of trauma and a nuanced portrait of a complex young woman trying to hold together her shattered personality for the cosy community which wishes her to conform to their ideals and never speak of her torment, or their complicity in it.

FWWM is a challenging film that assumes intelligence and curiosity on the part of its audience, as well as a compassion for all its characters: the possessed as well as the powerless. It leads the viewer on a difficult and disturbing journey, but despite the horror and tribulations it offers us a vision of peace after pain, and a belief that those who traverse the fire with a pure heart can be rewarded with a sublime salvation.

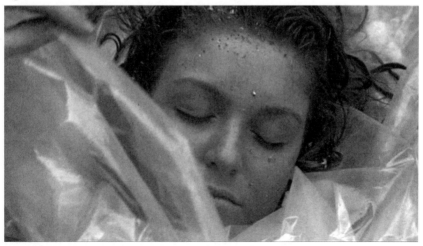

---

[5] Martha P. Nochimson, *The Passion of David Lynch: Wild at Heart in Hollywood* (Austin: University of Texas Press, 2012) Kindle Edition, location 155.

[6] Rodley, *Lynch on Lynch*, p. 32.

'The magician longs to see'

David Lynch

DAVID LYNCH WAS BORN IN MISSOULA, Montana on 20
January 1946, and within two months his family moved to
Sandpoint, Idaho. His father Donald worked for the US Government's
Department of Agriculture as a research scientist, and his mother Edwina
was a housewife. By the time he was fourteen David had lived in six
different parts of America; a brother John, and a sister Martha, rounded
out the Lynch household.

This childhood period of geographic displacement taught him techniques to adapt and to get along with people quickly. Even at that age he
figured out that being an outsider wasn't ideal when you were also the new
kid. The series of moves were a succession of disruptions, but he also
appreciated that they could open up opportunities for new experiences.

Lynch has repeatedly emphasised the idyllic quality of his boyhood
during a post-war era where, "You got the feeling you could do anything.
The future was bright."[7] Yet, there are signs that his upbringing had
some quirky characteristics. Lynch fondly recalls that his father always
wore a forest service ten-gallon hat with his suit, and forgoing a car or
bus, would walk several miles to work. It's typical of the kind of idiosyncratic detail that would become one of the hallmarks of a Lynchian
character. Both his parents were college educated, but his mother never
permitted him to use colouring books because she felt this was too
restricting.

---

[7] Rodley, *Lynch on Lynch*, p. 5.

Since his father was a research scientist who experimented with tree diseases and insects Lynch had been exposed to the teeming underbelly of nature all his life. Pitch oozed from pretty trees, and there were bugs under every rock. If you peeled back the top layer and delved far enough a different, primordial world would be revealed.

A suspicion began to arise in young Lynch's mind that the clear skies and white picket fences of his childhood were a type of illusion.

I learned that just beneath the surface there's another world, and still different worlds as you dig deeper. I knew it as a kid, but I couldn't find the proof. It was just a feeling. There is goodness in blue skies and flowers, but another force—a wild pain and decay—also accompanies everything.[8]

Through trips to visit family he began to observe that there were other, harsher environments that existed alongside his clean-cut world. His maternal grandparents lived in Brooklyn, New York. To a country boy the chaotic city was a roar and a trial.

He said: "In the subway I remember a wind from the approaching train, then a smell and a sound. I had a taste of horror every time I went to New York."[9] This association with wind and sound, a kind of roaring tinnitus, a shorthand for an agitated state, is an element that appears in many of Lynch's works—including the cut-scenes of tree branches shaken by a desolate wind that intersperse all of *Twin Peaks*.

In New York Lynch discovered that were no kitchens in the small apartments. On a metaphorical level, to a child from suburbia, this is the absence of the hearth and comfort. One day he saw "A man was cooking an egg on an iron—that really worried me." It's a perfect example of his ability to notice incongruous details—little elements that are out of synch with 'normal' everyday reality which stick in the mind. They are niggling signs that all is not right; the orderly world might be poised to descend into bedlam.

Depicting these disquieting disturbances within a seemingly placid

---

[8] Ibid., p. 8.

[9] Ibid., p. 8.

setting is a technique that Lynch employs often in his work to establish how easily a world can be destabilised.

On Lynch's official Twitter account he describes himself as "Filmmaker. Born Missoula, MT. Eagle Scout." This sparse description hints at what he considers crucial to his identity: his work, his birth in 'big sky country', and his interest in mastering hands-on, practical skills that requires a stubborn dedication to achieve a goal.

A typical Eagle Scout must earn 21 merit badges, demonstrate leadership and civic spirit, and complete an extensive service project. It can take years to earn, and only about 4% of Scouts ever attain the distinction. Lynch has said that when he was a boy scout it wasn't cool at all, but he persisted from a desire to "put it behind me."[10] His father told him he'd be proud of the achievement one day, so it has become Lynch's lone badge of honour on his resume. Yet, like his moving 1999 film, *The Straight Story*, it also serves as a reminder that Lynch understands how to navigate the standard norms of society—he just doesn't necessarily want to be bound by them.

Lynch's visual capacity developed first. He drew and painted all the time as a child, but he never conceived anyone could make a career as an artist until he met Bushnell Keeler, the father of his friend Roby, who was a professional painter. In the 9th grade David Lynch found his calling.

After he graduated high school, he started his studies at the School of the Museum of Fine Arts, Boston in 1964, but he was uninspired. He travelled for a time with his friend and fellow artist Jack Fisk, but returned home to odd jobs. In 1965 he moved to the city of Philadelphia to enrol at the Pennsylvania Academy of Fine Arts. Fisk was already attending the Academy and encouraged him.

He began a relationship with a fellow student, Peggy Reavey, and they were married in 1967. The following year, Peggy gave birth to their daughter Jennifer. They lived in the Fairmount neighbourhood of Philadelphia, where they bought a massive house for a knock-down price because it was in a tricky area. This period had a huge impact upon Lynch's imagination and later work.

---

[10] Ibid., p. 5.

He immersed himself and his young family in the lawless world that he had only glimpsed until then. To his surprise with the uneasiness came exhilaration.

We lived cheap, but the city was full of fear. A kid was shot to death down the street, and the chalk marks around where he'd lain stayed on the sidewalk for five days. We were robbed twice, had windows shot out and a car stolen. The house was first broken into only three days after we moved in . . .

I tell people that all that protected us from the outside were these bricks. But the bricks might as well have been paper. The feeling was so close to extreme danger, and the fear was so intense. There was violence and hate and filth. But the biggest influence in my whole life was that city. And it just happened at the perfect time. I saw things that were frightening, but more than that, thrilling.[11]

It was dramatically demonstrated to him that the safety of the home can be an illusion; forces underneath, or chaos from without, can batter down the domestic fortress. And that persistent danger can possess a magnetic, seductive charm. In this regard Lynch is like Jeffrey Beaumont (Kyle MacLachlan), the naïve protagonist of his 1986 film **Blue Velvet,** who is drawn into a dangerous, seedy world by his obsession with a damaged, beautiful woman.

It was while working on an almost all-black figurative painting that Lynch first had the idea of wanting to add sound and movement. Without any experience or notion about how to make a film he bought a 16mm wind-up camera and taught himself how to make an animated film. The project cost $200—which was hugely expensive from a student's point of view—and it resulted in **Six Men Getting Sick**, his first short film. The project took joint first prize at the Academy's end of year show. It's a crude depiction of six men disgorging in sequence accompanied by a taped loop of a siren shrieking. Despite its simplicity, it remains a discomforting film to watch today.

---

[11] Ibid., pp. 42-43

This might have been the end to Lynch's foray into film if it wasn't for a wealthy student called H. Barton 'Bart' Wasserman who offered Lynch the princely sum of $1,000 to create a similar film for him. Flush with cash, Lynch spent $450 on a Bolex camera, and set about teaching himself to use it. Within two months he had shot his film.

But once he developed it Lynch discovered the camera had a faulty part and the entire film was ruined. Inexplicably, Lynch describes being happy about this accident. He explained the problem to Bart, who encouraged Lynch to make something else instead. This resulted in *The Alphabet*, which went on to land him a grant from the American Film Institute, and cement his path as a filmmaker. With that money he created a 34-minute short film, *The Grandmother*, in 1970, which was his first collaboration with sound editor/designer Alan Splet.

This lead to Splet and him securing scholarships to the AFI's Centre for Advanced Film Studies, and Lynch left the city of his major inspiration and moved to L.A. He might have abandoned the dark industrial landscape for the light-saturated streets of California, but Philadelphia lingered as a major presence his subsequent debut feature film, *Eraserhead*.

A labour of love, Lynch began prepping for the film in 1971, shooting it in 1972, but it wasn't completed until 1977. During this time he split up with his wife, moved into the same building space as the *Eraserhead* set, completed another short film called 'The Amputee', and remarried.

Eraserhead was a black and white surrealist film whose weird sensibility made it an underground cult sensation. It follows a young man named Henry (Jack Nance) living in a desolate industrial city, who copes with forced fatherhood of an alien, deformed child, and is soothed by the Lady in the Radiator (Laurel Near) before and after the inevitable crisis of responsibility.

The Lady in the Radiator resides within a hidden world inside a mundane object, and sings to Henry from a stage swathed in curtains as she attempts to stamp out disgusting distractions. This is an early example of a key symbol: the theatrical stage that exists within the cinematic narrative. The singer channels the frustration and fears of the principal character through song, in a manner that the chief protagonist is incapable of doing. In this way s/he finds a kind of release, but often it is signals the onset of imminent danger.

Performance, masks, playing a part, hidden identities, and confused personalities will become major themes of much of Lynch's work and are apparent early. The film is also concerned with strange extra-dimensional entities that monitor/experiment upon people—which could be construed as diabolic or angelic.

It also features curtains and the zig-zag floor pattern which will appear again in Lynch's work. He admits, "I've got a thing about curtains and I don't know why, because I've never done any theatre. But I *love* curtains, and a place where you look and it's contained. I just really love it."[12] As is typical Lynch doesn't over-analyse his visual lexicography. He trusts that it works, and has meaning for him; after that the task is to employ it effectively.

Eraserhead had mixed critical reactions, and was rejected for screening at both the New York Film Festival and Cannes, but it became popular at midnight screenings in cinemas.

Lynch's next concept was for a film called **Ronnie Rocket**, which he pithily described to a studio executive as "about electricity and a three-foot guy with red hair."[13] Luckily, a young junior producer called Stuart Cornfeld had seen *Eraserhead,* and been hugely impressed by it. He tracked down Lynch, and they discussed projects, but even he couldn't sell *Ronnie Rocket.* It was Cornfeld who famously described Lynch as "Jimmy Stewart from Mars".[14]

Cornfeld suggested Lynch direct a film called **The Elephant Man**— Lynch loved the title and jumped at the chance without even knowing the subject matter. Lynch was a complete unknown in Hollywood, but Mel Brooks expressed interest in making *The Elephant Man* for his new production company BrooksFilms. The only hitch was he wanted to view *Eraserhead* before he gave the directing gig to Lynch. At this point Lynch figured he had lost his chance, but after watching the movie Brooks exclaimed to Lynch: "You're a madman, I love you! You're in."[15]

---

[12] Ibid., p. 187.

[13] Ibid., p. 91.

[14] Ibid., p. xii.

[15] Ibid., p. 93.

The screenplay was adapted by Lynch, Christopher De Vore, and Eric Bergren from Frederick Treves's *The Elephant Man and Other Reminiscences* (1923) and Ashley Montagu's *The Elephant Man: A Study in Human Dignity* (1971). It was shot in black-and-white, and Christopher Tucker created the prosthetic make-up. Up until this point Lynch had been a one-man DIY filmmaker who had taught himself every aspect of the craft to realise his vision. For *The Elephant Man* he had a large budget, an experienced crew, a cast of award-winning British actors, with a historical 19th century setting, plus he had to shoot it in London. It was a daunting challenge for a relatively untried American director, but Brooks threw his full support behind Lynch and advocated for him strongly, and that was instrumental in helping Lynch adapt to the change.

The film follows the story of John Merrick (Joseph Merrick in real life), played by John Hurt, a man with extreme physical deformities who was rescued from being exhibited at a freak show as the 'Elephant Man' by Dr Frederick Treves (Anthony Hopkins). John keeps a photo of his mother always to hand so she's a presence throughout the narrative, and appears in a tangible way at the end of the film. Not only is Merrick reunited with her loving presence, accompanied by the sound of wind and *Adagio in Strings*, and the assurance that 'Nothing will die,' but the audience is similarly comforted and transported to a place of hope and care despite the death of the story's hero.

Merrick is tortured because his unusual appearance does not reflect the spirit within, and he is forced to perform a simplistic caricature of how others perceive him. The freak show doesn't exhibit the people within the carnival, but the character of those who wish to exploit them, and the punters who gape at them. Merrick's deformity is hidden from the audience for a long period—often by curtains, or a bag[16]—partly to enhance suspense and offer a dramatic reveal, but also to remind the audience of its symbiotic voyeurism. We wish *to see*. Yet with Merrick, there is a lot more to be discovered than his peculiar physiognomy.

---

[16] In typical Lynchian style, the rough cloth hood with the lone eyehole evokes a disturbing dread, even when it hangs from a hook. It is a container for Victorian society's deep revulsion for difference.

The film is astutely directed with fine performances and a straight-forward narrative. There are harrowing moments of cruelty and torture as Merrick's disability not only casts him as an outsider, but also increases his vulnerability. But it is the emotional anguish that is the most crushing, and Lynch is particularly adept at evoking those intangible internal crises, especially with an actor whose face is obscured. The most surreal moments in the film are restricted to the opening scene where an Elephant appears to trample and possess Merrick's mother, and the final moment of reunification. Yet this is a trademark Lynchian narrative: an alienated protagonist, curtained areas, performances and performers, hissing pipes, and a filthy world that is parallel to the cleaner (but not morally superior) realm of 'civilisation'.

The Elephant Man was a critical and commercial success, earned eight Academy Award nominations, and three BAFTAS. The only award it won was a César Award; a harbinger of the French love affair with Lynch's films.

The classic career trajectory for an American director is that after a small, successful film the big-budget plum gets offered, and in this case Italian film producer Dino De Laurentiis came calling with the offer to adapt Frank Herbert's dense science fiction novel, **Dune**. De Laurentiis had not seen *Eraserhead* when he offered Lynch the job, so he may not have been aware of the entire range of Lynch's aesthetic (and when he did watch the movie De Laurentiis hated it). It was the chance for Lynch to explore several unusual worlds, but the film came with all the complication and oversight of an expensive production, and compared to Lynch's previous two films, it was on a monumental scale.

The project consumed three of Lynch's creative years, with one of them focused strictly on reworking the script: he worked extensively with Frank Herbert on an almost line-by-line discussion of the novelist's intentions for his characters and settings, and then in script development with his co-writers from *The Elephant Man*: De Vore and Bergren. The script-writing did not proceed harmoniously, and the trio parted ways when they could not agree on the film's vision. Of that experience Lynch said: "A writer is like a filter: the ideas pass through his personal artistic screen before they hit the paper. *Dune*'s notions came from Frank's book, but I interpreted them."[17]

---

[17] Rodley, *Lynch on Lynch*, p. 115.

It's difficult to summarise simply how the project went sideways, but most importantly for Lynch he did not feel in creative control of the project. It was shot in Mexico and there were eight huge sound studios, which were filled to twice their capacity with sets, and Lynch continually made concessions that affected his relationship to the film. The integrity of the complex narrative could not withstand the brutal whittling down from its initial four-hour rough cut to the just over two-hour theatrical release. Lynch later understood where he erred:

> I didn't really feel I had permission to really make it my own. That was the downfall for me. It was a problem. Dune was like a kind of studio film. I didn't have final cut. And, little by little, I was subconsciously making compromises—knowing that I couldn't go here and not wanting to go there. I just fell, you know, into this middle world. It was a sad place to be.[18]

Yet, there are aspects of the film to admire, from its outlandish design and the performances of many of the actors, including the first appearance of a young Kyle MacLachlan as Paul Atreides, the son of a Duke with mystical powers who is involved in an inter-planetary internecine feud over a vital commodity, Spice, which is produced only on one planet. Today, it would be referred to as *Game of Thrones* in Space.[19]

The frustrating aspect of watching *Dune* is sensing all that is missing. There are plenty of elements that resonant with Lynch's usual fare, including the charge "The sleeper must awaken", and the presence of the corrupting and corpulent Baron Vladimir Harkonnen (Kenneth McMillan) who preys upon the good. Yet none of it can save what is an incomplete and unsatisfactory film.

Dune, released in 1984, was a commercial and critical failure, an inverse *The Elephant Man*: outrageous colour and fantastical design compared to

---

[18] Ibid., pp. 119-120.

[19] The lasting appeal of the books means that it was subsequently adapted by the SyFy channel into two mini-series: *Dune* (2000) and *Children of Dune* (2003), which had different problems than Lynch's version. Director Denis Villeneuve is tipped to bring the story back to the big screen, but least two other directors have recently attempted and failed to make it work. The source material does not navigate easily to film.

stark black and white realism, a complex story in the future spanning a tribal universe versus the quiet tale of people desiring possession of an invalid man in Victorian London. Yet *The Elephant Man* proved that Lynch had the capacity to produce elegiac work, and he acknowledged subsequently that it saved his reputation from complete ruin.

Lessons learned, Lynch returned to what he does best: an examination of the dangers that lurk behind the suburban façade: *Blue Velvet* (1986). It's the film that presages *Twin Peaks*, and it reunited him with MacLachlan as Jeffrey, the young man who discovers an entire new aspect to the world, and himself. Jeffrey stumbles upon a severed ear—he listens to the mystery it tells—and is lead to a pretty co-detective Sandy Williams (Laura Dern), who shares his voyeuristic tendencies. Through this he discovers the tormented lady in blue, Dorothy Vallens (Isabella Roselli), a crooner who is the singing, caged bird for the rapacious and sadistic criminal, Frank Booth (Denis Hopper).

The opening scene of the film sets out its visual language clearly with the dreamy 'Blue Velvet' playing, sung by Bobby Vinton. It's shot low, with the blue sky seen first, followed by a white picket fence with bright red roses planted before it. Red is always a sign of danger or warning in Lynch's films. An old-fashioned red fire truck sails by with an obedient Dalmatian sitting beside the fireman, who waves in welcome. There's a Norman Rockwell quality to this idealised vision of small town America, but its heightened reality is eerie, not comforting. The picket fence returns but with yellow tulips, some of which are wilting. One of the older meanings for yellow flowers was to represent jealousy or infidelity, and it's an abrupt colour shift. This is followed by children crossing a street with a stark red 'Stop' sign facing the audience. The warnings are clear: love will transform, and bring danger.

This is followed by Mr Beaumont watering his lawn to maintain the perfection of his house and setting (the most American of activities), and a new sound emerges as his hose tangles: a chittering underneath the dreamy song. Inside the house, his wife watches a black and white noir film, in which a gun is foregrounded, almost emerging from the screen. The home is invaded. Beaumont has a heart attack, while a toddler and dog (symbols of innocence and a feral nature) ignore his peril. And underneath it all, in the grass, the unnerving sound swells, and there are ants, busy with their own alien agenda.

Within a couple of minutes Lynch has signalled his intentions, but this is not clear to the critical mind upon first viewing: but an older instinct understands, and it puts the audience on edge. And it's warranted: *Blue Velvet* remains a challenging film with violent and sexually fraught scenes that continue to shock thirty years after its release. Jeffry is both stalker and victim, sadist and saviour, and he is introduced to the mystery by Sandy, whose world is undermined by Jeffrey's investigations. There are few cinematic villains as arresting and intimidating as Frank Booth, and yet there are intimations of his yearning for love, however he twists it. And Dorothy is the broken, resilient woman, desperate for goodness, but unable to trust anything but pain.

The seeds of Agent Dale Cooper are also evident in the film when Jeffrey plays detective, especially in the scenes when he lays it all out for Sandy and her police officer father.

It's a tremendous, striking piece of cinema, and hugely aided by the beginning of Lynch's collaboration with composer Angelo Badalamenti. The aural landscapes of Lynch's films had always been exemplary, but in cooperation with Badalamenti's lush score *Blue Velvet* was elevated to a masterclass of filmmaking.

Blue Velvet, Twin Peaks, and *FWWM*, could be summarised by an understanding Lynch came to as a child: "The home is a place where things can go wrong."[20]

His experience in Philadelphia demonstrated to him that homes can be breached, and murderers walk the same streets as regular folk — and occasionally those paths intersect.

The film was a critical hit and a modest commercial success, but it redeemed Lynch's reputation which had been hammered by *Dune*. All the potential of the director of *The Elephant Man* came to fruition in a disturbing examination of human life. It was extensively nominated for prizes, and won 18 across various festivals and awards ceremonies.

Cinema goers learned that Lynch could render the familiar both strange and upsetting, but he also offered hope and comfort. There are no

---

[20] Rodley, *Lynch on Lynch*, p. 10.

easy solutions or neat endings in his work, but instead there are new understandings, and an appreciation for the paradox of existence.

As he said: "if one looks a little closer at this beautiful world, there are always red ants underneath."[21]

And in *Twin Peaks*, he helped create an entire ant colony to observe.

'One chance out between two worlds'

Twin Peaks

L YNCH'S PARTNERSHIP WITH Mark Frost came about in the usual fashion in Hollywood: a movie needed to be made and someone put the two creatives in a room. Frost was an experienced playwright and screenwriter with a strong reputation for his work on TV serials such as *The Six Million Dollar Man* and *Hill Street Blues*. He was keen to adapt Anthony Summer's *Goddess: The Secret Lives of Marilyn Monroe* (1985) into a film. Lynch was suggested as the director. The woman in peril idea appealed to Lynch, but he "didn't know if liked it being a real story."[22]

While this project made the studio rounds they also wrote a comedy together called **One Saliva Bubble**, which FWWM co-writer Robert Engels described thus: "It's about an electric bubble from a computer that bursts over this town and changes people's personalities—like these five cattlemen, who suddenly think that they're Chinese gymnasts. It's insane!"[23] Neither project survived the Hollywood obstacle course, but it cemented a friendship and creative collaboration between the two men. The latter concept is a reminder that Frost can mine a deep seam of whimsy, something which often gets unilaterally attributed to Lynch. Lynch notes that they complement each other creatively, and "he always understood what I was saying. Maybe he helped bring me into more of a real world."[24]

---

[22] Rodley, *Lynch on Lynch*, p. 156.

[23] Ibid., p. 155.

[24] Ibid., p. 162.

At this time Lynch's agent Tony Krantz tried to engage Lynch with the idea of writing for television. Lynch turned to his recent collaborator Frost—who was intimately familiar with this demanding medium—to toss around a few ideas.

As Lynch recalled they were in a coffee shop when they "had this image of a body washing up on the shore of a lake."[25] The town of *Twin Peaks* and its murder mystery storyline quickly snowballed. Initially the faraway Great Plains in North Dakota was chosen as the setting, but the thickly forested landscape of the north-west coast of America, tight to the Canadian border (an in-between space), won out in their imaginations.

The show's first title was *Northwest Passage*, but it changed to the name of the town that would become a crucible for strangeness. Lynch recollected their core concept:

> *The mystery of who killed Laura Palmer was the foreground, but this would recede slightly as you got to know the other people in the town and the problems they were having. And each week would feature close-ups of some things. The project was to mix a police investigation with the ordinary lives of the characters. We had drawn a map of the town. We knew where everything was located and helped us determine the prevailing atmosphere and what might happen there. I guess what made* Twin Peaks Twin Peaks *is hard to talk about. I don't think we even know what it was. But ABC said they wanted to do the pilot.*[26]

There are many pilots that are never successfully commissioned as a fully-fledged TV series, so when Lynch and Frost got the go-ahead for their test episode they were filled with the "euphoria of 'this probably isn't going to go anywhere, let's really do it.'"[27]

They worked off a comprehensive feature-length script, co-written by Frost and Lynch, but several novel elements that are important to the allure of the TV series didn't evolve until Lynch was directing on location

[25] Ibid., p. 157.

[26] Ibid., p. 158.

[27] Ibid., p. 159.

at the Snoqualmie Valley of Washington State, and later in post-produc-tion, which is typical of Lynch's instinctive approach to filmmaking.

> *Here's the deal—something isn't finished until it's finished. When you start focusing on something, [it] gets a kind of an energy going and things begin to flow. But ideas don't come when you just snap your fingers. They come along out of who-knows-what. But there is this focus that pulls them, I think. I always say, "You should always be aware." You might think your script is complete but it may not be. There may be opportunities and ideas coming that are so valuable. You have to stay feeling [it], and focused all the time. Lots of things will start talking to you. It's just the way. It's got to all feel correct to be finished. You've just got to be with it.*[28]

One of the famous lightning-strike moments of inspiration that was a turning point for the series is the hiring of Frank Silva in the role of BOB, the diabolical entity that possesses and stalks certain inhabitants of Twin Peaks. Silva was working on the show as the set dresser when he was moving a chest-of-drawers through the doorway of Laura Palmer's bedroom, and someone warned him "Frank, don't lock yourself in the room."[29] Lynch saw Silva in that moment, behind the piece of furniture, and knew he had to put him into the show, though Lynch had no idea what Silva's role would be. True to his method of creating work, Lynch didn't second-guess his instinct. Considering the importance of BOB as the antagonising force in the series it was a significant, late addition.

The Red Room and its occupants didn't occur to Lynch until he was edit-ing the pilot back in L.A. He was leaving the editing room for the evening, and placed his hands upon the roof of a warm car, and "The Red Room scene leapt into my mind. 'Little Mike' was there and he was speaking backwards."[30] Lynch had previously met actor Mike Anderson, who would play The Man From Another Place in *Twin Peaks*, when Lynch was planning *Ronnie Rocket*.

---

[28] John Thorne, *The Essential Wrapped in Plastic: Pathways to Twin Peaks* (John Thorne, 2016). Kindle edition, location 6075.

[29] Rodley, *Lynch on Lynch*, p. 163.

[30] Ibid., p. 165.

Due to their late conception, neither of the mysterious extra-dimensional entities BOB or the Man From Another Place feature significantly in the pilot episode, which is a surprise considering how much they, and the Red Room, became integral to the storylines in *Twin Peaks*. But Lynch had a contractual obligation to complete a version of the pilot for the European market that offered a solution to the murder. In a couple of days he filmed an expository coda for the pilot, which was later re-purposed as Cooper's dream sequence at the end of episode two. It provided important background information, and involved the One Armed Man (MIKE) confessing to his rivalry with BOB, the first recital of the 'Fire Walk With Me' poem, a mound of earth surrounded by candles, and the debut of the Red Room. These are all elements that achieve a fuller explanation in the series and the feature length film, and indicate that on some level Lynch was prepping for *FWWM* for a long time.

The actress Sheryl Lee, who played Laura Palmer (primarily a corpse in the pilot), was noticed because they needed a local actress for the part, and she worked in Seattle. It was not until Lynch began filming Lee that he understood her natural potential. This inspired Lynch to give her another role when the TV series was greenlit, and she became Laura's cousin, Maddy Ferguson.[31] In this way Laura Palmer's spirit literally haunted the town as a metaphor for its guilt and secrets via Maddie's visible presence. This tension would eventually result in a breaking point where reality and unreality collapsed, provoking Laura Palmer's killer to murder again.

The shooting of the ninety-minute pilot was uniformly described by all those involved in the show as a blissful period, despite the freezing temperatures during February–March 1989 and their sparse motel accommodation. The resulting piece of work, full of charm, grief, and sinister forces at play under the Mom and Pop vernacular, both beguiled and puzzled ABC executives. It was reported by *Variety* that one of them described it as "Norman Rockwell meets Salvador Dali"[32], and they

---

[31] In several scenes in *Twin Peaks* Maddy wears a fluffy blue robe, which had a large flower motif on one side—perhaps the earliest, sly reference to the blue rose mystery.

[32] David Bushman & Arthur Smith, *Twin Peaks FAQ: All That's Left to Know About a Place Both Wonderful and Strange* (Milwaukee: Applause Theatre & Cinema Books, 2016), p. 4.

weren't confident that American audiences would watch a murder mystery set in a Washington state town with a European surrealist vibe.[33]

Yet it was 1989, a new decade was over the horizon, and television was changing. Staples such as *Moonlighting, Family Ties, Miami Vice,* and *Dynasty* all ended that year, and among the new shows being ordered there were signs of a shift in interest, with *The Simpsons, Seinfeld, Quantum Leap, The Arsenio Hall Show, Alien Nation* and *Tales From the Crypt* debuting.[34]

Frost and Lynch pushed hard to get their show greenlit, and word leaked out about the creative duo and their compelling pilot. Interest sparked, and ABC eventually ordered another seven episodes for one-hour slots, so *Twin Peaks* would fill in as a mid-season replacement. The cast and crew re-assembled joyfully, and shot the first season from October–December in 1989.

Lynch and Frost had plenty of time to work and break down the extra seven episodes of the first season, but Lynch only co-wrote the first and second episodes with Frost, and directed the second one. After that Lynch was prepping for his next feature film, **Wild at Heart**, co-starring Laura Dern and Nicolas Cage, in an energetic road movie which Lynch had adapted from a novel by Barry Gifford. Frost acted as showrunner in Lynch's absence, and tapped newcomers Harley Peyton and Robert Engels for writing duties to help out—they ended up being significant contributors to the entire show.

The pilot for *Twin Peaks* aired on 8 April 1990 to a huge audience—35 million viewers—and immediately became a sensation with rave reviews. The numbers dropped off to an average of around 19 million until the broadcast of the first season finale, 'The Last Evening', on 23 May, and the cliffhanger moment of the shooting of Agent Dale Cooper.

Two days later *Wild at Heart* debuted at the Cannes Film Festival to an enthusiastic reception, and went on to win the prestigious Palme d'Or.

---

[33] Today, that would be a selling point for a Netflix series, and is an indicator of how much *Twin Peaks* changed the landscape of American television.

[34] Along with signs of the ramping up of 'reality' TV in the form of *Cops* and *Rescue 911*, and the continuation of classic family fare, with the likes of *Baywatch* and *Dougie Howser, M.D.* first airing on television.

The world seemed at Lynch and Frost's feet[35]: the media loved their work and their zany characters, and the fans of the show proved themselves to be ardent and loyal. In an era long before cosplay, fans dressed up as their favourite characters for *Twin Peaks* viewings, and they were desperate for any merchandise.[36]

There were many elements that contributed to the success of the show, including the memorable characters, startling storylines, offbeat style, retro design, and beautiful theme music and score by Badalamenti, but also the wealth of details, many of which seemed essential to ponder further. This was a deliberate decision by Frost, who has stated:

> *[I] wanted to include what became known as 'Easter eggs' in the video game industry a few years later, where people would be rewarded for heightened scrutiny of what they were seeing. You would see that in character's names or in relationships or pieces of casting.*
>
> *Honestly, I didn't know if anyone would ever notice, but it was certainly fun for us to do. Waldo [the myna bird] was a reference to Waldo Lydecker who was one of the principle characters in [the Otto Preminger film] Laura, as is Laura for that matter.[37]*

It was a prescient move by Frost, and allusions that were oblique in the short first season were padded out in the second season by various writers, and a deeper mythology about the town, its landscape, and its denizens began to evolve and expand. As Dennis Lim notes, *"Twin Peaks* was a mass-culture text that called for communal decoding, a semiotic wonderland of clues, symbols, and red herrings."[38]

---

[35] *Twin Peaks* was nominated for a staggering fourteen Emmys that year, but only won two—for editing and costume design.

[36] Two tie-ins were hugely popular: the audiobook *'Diane'... The Twin Peaks Tapes of Agent Cooper* performed by MacLachlan (he was nominated for a Grammy Award for best spoken-word performance), and *The Secret Diary of Laura Palmer*, written by Jennifer Lynch, which hit the *New York Times* best seller list.

[37] Brad Dukes, *Reflections: An Oral History of Twin Peaks* (Short/Tall Press, 2014). Kindle edition, location 971.

[38] Dennis Lim, *David Lynch: The Man from Another Place* (Icons) (New Harvest, 2015), Kindle edition, location 1463.

The other factor to consider about *Twin Peaks'* popularity is that it was released at a time when the video recorder had hit widespread saturation. Viewers could record the show, and re-watch it obsessively with fellow fans while hunting for clues about hidden meaning through slowed down scenes and freeze frame. TV had moved away from being akin to the temporal pleasure of theatre, where if you were not present in your living room at curtain up you had to make peace with the fact that you would never see it again, except in a rumoured re-run.

Television had entered a new phase of being consumed on-demand, and it would start to alter how people viewed their shows. The worry was no longer that you might miss your programme, but that your video recorder was set up correctly, or if the tape had enough room for each episode. Even if that failed, a friend or relative was sure to have recorded it, and tapes could be exchanged. *Twin Peaks* benefited immensely from this paradigm shift in viewership. Fans could 'own' the fascinating series in a way that encouraged forensic examination.

It's also worth noting that *Twin Peaks* was developed and aired during a seismic political shift—the Cold War thaw. US President Ronald Reagan left office in 1989, and later that year the Berlin Wall fell and was dismantled: a staggering event with consequences that reverberated around the world. In 1990 Germany reunified and British Prime Minister Margaret Thatcher bowed out as head of state. The following year, the USSR itself collapsed.

It was a sudden, shocking lurch of direction as the 1990s began, with the second millennium no longer a distant prospect. The pervading threat of nuclear extermination, which had hovered as a possibility throughout the 1980s, was replaced with a sense of political evolution and personal optimism. The world was not without problems and crisis, but in the Western world the old enemies had changed. Something new was necessary.

Twin Peaks reflected that. With its cosy diner, gas station, lumber mill, and hotel at the centre of the town's economy, it harkened back to the 1950s post-war small-town comfortableness, but from the start that was a flimsy facade covering challenging problems (One-Eyed Jack's, the nearby Canadian brothel, was the dark secret outlet for some of the town's citizens). There were genuine brutalities in Twin Peaks. Laura Palmer, the town's murdered sweetheart, was discovered to have been doing drugs and involved in a wide array of sexual experiences. There were shady business practices, drug deals, domestic abuse, Asian assassins, love triangles, arson, escaped lunatics, and murder plots. There was also a sprinkling of true love. And the gradual revelation of the town as a spiritual nexus point, where supernatural forces clashed for possession of the souls of the residents.

Its first engine was "Who killed Laura Palmer?" That became the refrain of the show, and people were desperate to discover the murderer[39], with it being a popular topic for water cooler conversations. Media speculation was so intense about the identity of the killer that Randy Barbee (*Twin Peaks* series assistant director) reported:

We *had* National Enquirer *reporters going through our dumpsters trying to find old script pages. They were putting out numbered scripts with your particular number and if a photocopy showed up with your number somewhere, you were basically out of a job.*[40]

When *Twin Peaks* was optioned for a second season of 22 episodes the creators no longer had any breathing space to develop the stories, and hired more writers and directors to take up the slack.[41] They also came under increasing pressure to reveal the killer of Laura Palmer, something Lynch and Frost never intended doing so quickly, but early in the second season they bowed to the pressure from executives, media, and fans.

Lynch directed only four episodes of the second season of *Twin Peaks*: the first, second, and final episodes, and the pivotal seventh episode, 'Lonely Souls', which was written by Frost, in which Laura's killer was finally revealed in a shockingly violent scene.

---

[39] Lynch and Frost kept the killer's identity as a tight secret, only a tiny number of people knew, and no one in ABC had been told.

[40] Duke, *Reflections*, location 1726.

[41] Both Lynch and Frost had less time available for *Twin Peaks* in season two, but all the extra writers credited Frost with being highly involved in oversight of the scripts. Lynch was involved in promoting *Wild at Heart* and Frost was prepping for *Storyville*.

To maintain secrecy, they shot the crucial moment—in which Laura's cousin Maddy was brutally murdered—in three different ways. Sheryl Lee endured a twelve-hour shoot in which her character was killed by BOB, then by Benjamin Horne (Richard Beymer), the local business magnate, and finally by Leland Palmer (Ray Wise), Laura's father. None of them knew who the killer was when they were put through their punishing paces.

Viewing figures for *Twin Peaks* had been dropping in the second season after the first episode, but when ABC announced Laura's murderer would be revealed it jumped up to 17 million. In a mesmerising, gripping television experience, Leland was revealed as an incestuous killer. The full understanding of the abuse Laura had endured stunned American audiences, and they recoiled.

Without its central mystery *Twin Peaks* required a new narrative spine, and it slumped until Windom Earle (Kenneth Welsh) emerged as the main villain late in the series. By the second part of the second season the show was increasingly propped up by manic antics, and was in danger of becoming a pastiche of itself. It's a testament to the delicate line between stylised drama and exaggerated farce that Lynch and Frost navigated in their work that the new writers and directors often struggled to replicate it.

In the first season a fictional soap opera, *Invitation to Love*, is watched by several *Twin Peaks* residents, and it functioned as a cheerful ironic commentary on the format. By season two, some *Twin Peaks* episodes could have slotted in perfectly to that parody series. Season two included a misguided Miss Twin Peaks contest, and the agonising sight of Agent Cooper wearing a plaid shirt and practising fly fishing in his hotel room. Lynch, ever cognisant of the importance of symbols, wasn't pleased with this turn:

In the second season, Cooper ceased to be 100 per cent Cooperage for me. He got these flannel shirts and stuff! Some people maybe liked it. So you say, 'Yes, I'm glad in a way, and in another way I'm really sorry because a guy that's too much like me cannot sustain that intense interest or dream. He's got to be specific. Cooper is a certain way. It's necessary.' If you start seeing the Queen of England going around in a Volkswagen or something, it doesn't make it. It's gotta be a Rolls-Royce. That's what you want.[42]

Appropriately, it's David Lynch playing FBI Regional Bureau Chief Gordon Cole, who puts a stop to that nonsense in the episode 'On the Wings of Love'. Cooper dons his iconic outfit again, and returns to his role as FBI agent.

But it was too late. Like Cooper, *Twin Peaks* had suffered an identity crisis, and in the eyes of ABC it was fatal. The show had always been a long punt on a strange dream, and the viewing figures indicated a failure of faith in the vision. By the end of the second season at its worst it plummeted to 7.4 million viewers, and only rose to 10.4 million for the last two episodes.

Lynch returned to direct the final episode, 'Beyond Life and Death', which had been scripted by Mark Frost, Harley Peyton, and Robert Engels. Its main action is the abduction of Annie Blackburn (Heather Graham), Cooper's girlfriend, by the master of disguise and nefarious Windom Earle, just after Annie's been crowned Miss Twin Peaks. Her designation as a 'Queen' grants her a symbolic power that allows Earle to use her to open a passage to the Black Lodge via the portal at Glastonbury Grove.

Lynch stuck to the script as it was written until it came to the infamous Red Room sequence, during which Cooper enters the Black Lodge in pursuit of Earle and Annie, and ends up in a fight with his own shadow self. He said that part was "completely and totally wrong."[43]

He threw away the pages, and shot most of it on-the-spot to his understanding of that realm. Considering it was Lynch who first conceived of the Red Room, it was correct for him to keep it aligned with his artistic vision. It's an extraordinary piece of television, with past mistakes and the dead haunting the space, entities fighting for control of souls (Earle loses that battle), and Cooper being defeated by his doppelganger self.

As becomes clearer in *Fire Walk With Me*, only those with the right

---

[42] Rodley, *Lynch on Lynch*, p. 182.

[43] Ibid., p. 182.

intentions survive the purgatory fire of the Red Room. Cooper, unprepared and gunning after Earle, is not ready to face the hardest struggle: with the darker instincts in himself.

The last image of Cooper, returned from the Lodge as a vessel for BOB, bloodied and giggling in his hotel room, was a shocking final moment without any hope of further resolution since the show was cancelled. Many fans yearned for a sequel, and when news hit that Lynch planned a spin-off film, many people believed they would finally have all the answers they craved.

Except, that was never Lynch's motivation:

At the end of the series, I felt sad. I couldn't get myself to leave the world of Twin Peaks. I was in love with the character of Laura Palmer and her contradictions: radiant on the surface but dying inside. I wanted to see her live, move and talk. I was in love with that world I hadn't finished with it. But making the movie wasn't just to hold on to it: it seemed that there was more stuff that could be done.[44]

Frost had no interest on working on a sequel to the series:

I was not involved at all. David and I had a disagreement about what direction a movie should go. I felt very strongly that our audience wanted to see the story go forward. So I declined to be involved in the movie.[45]

Lynch had been working with Robert Engels on various projects, including a script for a film called **In Heaven**. When he struck a three-picture deal with production company CIBY-2000, he asked Engels to co-write a prequel for *Twin Peaks* with him. Engels, who was completely familiar with the *Twin Peaks* universe, agreed.

Through long conversations and many drafts they worked to fashion the shooting script of *FWWM*, during which Engels helped Lynch open up the strange events that precipitated the TV series. Engels said:

---

[44] Ibid., p. 184.

[45] Thorne, *The Essential Wrapped in Plastic*, Kindle edition, location 5825.

It was a prequel and that was the whole idea. We didn't think about jumping forward again, that was never part of the discussion. It's just kind of a dream. There were too many things we all talked about that would've really made it go longer! It was the opposite of closure, rather than tie it up in a neat bow.[46]

They created a spec, and combined with the critical regard for the TV series, CIBY greenlit the film. *Twin Peaks: Fire Walk With Me* swung into production on 5 September 1991.

But at its première at Cannes in May 1992 it was met with the inverse reaction of the triumph of *Wild At Heart* two summers earlier.

Fire Walk With Me was the trip to the Red Room no one expected.

---

[46] Brad D. Studios, "Exclusive Interview with *Twin Peaks* screenwriter and producer, Bob Engels!" on http://braddstudios.com

'Fire Walk With Me'

I

IT'S WORTH STARTING a consideration of Lynch's *Twin Peaks* prequel feature film with the basics: the title itself, *Twin Peaks: Fire Walk With Me*[47]. The instruction, 'Fire Walk With Me', is initially shown in the pilot episode of *Twin Peaks*. When one compares the pilot of *Twin Peaks* with *Fire Walk With Me* it is notable how well they fit together, and how many of the important elements of the feature film are laid down in the first flowering of the mystery. Much of the extra layers of mythology that appear in the TV series, especially after Leland Palmer's death in the second season, are absent from Lynch's prequel.

The expression FIRE WALK WITH ME is first depicted written in blood, in capital letters, on a scrap of lined paper. It's discovered at the scene of Laura Palmer's murder: inside a derelict, rotting train carriage, hedged in by trees and trammelled by rusty, unused rail tracks. It is a place of stasis where nothing fulfils its function. The compartments are not attached to an engine, they no longer move, and the tracks go nowhere. It is the typical broken space that Lynch uses consistently in his work—its original purpose has been thwarted, and that makes it accessible for alien and unsettling energies.

---

[47] The full title of the shooting draft of the screenplay is: *Twin Peaks: Fire Walk With Me, Teresa Banks and the Last Seven Days of Laura Palmer*. The explicit mention of Teresa Banks serves to highlight that the focus of this film is on those who were left voiceless in *Twin Peaks* the TV series.

The cutting was dropped at the bottom of the mound of earth, on which sits half of a heart locket worn by Laura Palmer, an expression of her wish to be the girl that her secret boyfriend James Hurley wants her to be. It's also a perfect symbol of her shattered identity, and a literal example that some other person is always in possession of a piece of her.

Forensics eventually reveal that Laura's father wrote the summoning phrase in his blood. This mound of earth is seen in both the pilot and the feature film, and it always has an offering placed on top: an artefact of emotional or spiritual power that may open a portal to another world of understanding.

The depiction of the phrase in the pilot (and feature film) is a clue. Lynch is so particular about visual elements that this must be a deliberate decision. Fire is written larger, on top of a line so it seems underscored, and above the subsequent 'walk with me'—which is written in an almost run-on fashion. They are not parallel, but written at angles to one another, as if on a collision course. The emphasis is clear: Fire is what is being summoned, and it is the activating energy to facilitate the conjuror's journey. It could be written as 'Fire, walk with me'.

The alternative understanding of the phrase is that 'Fire Walk' is a path or trial that the petitioner is enjoining someone else to partake in. This is 'Fire walk, with me'.

This distinction is crucial. In one the invoker is calling upon Fire as a possessive spirit that will guide or power the conjuror's actions, and in the other it is an invitation to a shared path. All indications in the TV series, as in the film, point toward the first meaning.

One example where it is made clear is when Leland Palmer/BOB has been tricked into imprisonment in the Sheriff's Department in the *Twin Peaks* episode 'Arbitrary Law', and Cooper, Sheriff Harry Truman (Michael Ontkean), Deputy Hawk (Michael Horse), Agent Rosenfeld, as well as Benjamin Horne, watch voyeuristically from the cell door as BOB manifests in his full fury.

Leland/BOB repeats the poem, but with an additional stanza:

Through the dark of future's past
The magician longs to see

One chance out between two worlds
Fire walk with me.

I'll catch you in my death bag
You may think I've gone insane
But I promise, I will kill again

In this scene actor Ray Wise shouts "Fire!"—a typical cry of alarm—
with a pause, and then chews out "walk with me."

In this fashion the title of the feature film is its own summoning spell of
power, which I'll demonstrate brings wildness and strangeness, and is not
easily understood or controlled. As I've already outlined, Lynch's filmmaking style is to create a world of mystery and enfold the viewer into it,
often without clear guidelines. He does not do this to be oblique or frustrating, but because he wants to create dangerous possibilities that
transport the audience. This can result in unsettling or downright uncomfortable viewing.

Much of Lynch's cinema is designed to unbalance the viewers so their
perception is realigned with his dark, reimagined world.

II

*F*WWM opens with a screen of blue static, over a mood saxophone, which is part of the film score composed by Badalamenti. Static is a sign of a lost signal, but it also implies that the channel is awaiting reception. From the beginning, Lynch starts with the idea of hunting for a carrying signal, but as will be depicted in the film, care must be taken when choosing one's connection.

The titles are bold, white, and no-nonsense, and combined with the music the opening evokes the legacy of American noir thrillers — where terrible events befall innocents and villains alike, and a happy ending is not guaranteed. If anything, the elegiac melody hints at a tragic outcome.

All the actors and important crew members are given their credits up front, extending this mournful atmosphere, and lending the feeling of it already being the end of the movie. It suggests that what is going to happen next is out of bounds, that these events are beyond the TV series, set in their own special liminal space. It is one of the adjacent rooms to the *Twin Peaks* universe, and Lynch has set his will in motion to open the way.

As the titles end and Lynch's directorial credit appears the camera pulls back, and it's clear it has been tightly focused on a TV screen playing static. Lynch's subtle hint that events will not proceed in the fashion of the TV series is suddenly, brutally made overt when a huge hammer demol-

34

ishes the television set in an explosion of light and a crackle of electricity, along with a woman's scream of terror. Fire and electricity, Lynch's typical signs of disruption and transformation, wake up the viewer who has been lulled by the soothing opening music.

A form passes in front of the camera, and a woman's voice cries out "No!", followed by a wet thump. It has the dreadful sound of a killing blow.

This opening, which alternatively relaxes and jolts, warns of similar see-saws in pace to come. It's not described in the screenplay, but was devised later, no doubt to do exactly what it accomplishes: to demolish expectations.

After a fade to black the next scene opens on a tranquil river, edged with fir trees, with a body, wrapped in plastic, floating upon it. The words 'TERESA BANKS' appears, and with efficient storytelling Lynch indicates that this is the victim of the murder that has been overheard.

A swift cut reveals FBI Regional Bureau Chief Gordon Cole standing in front of a wall covered in a huge decal of a tranquil scene from the Pacific North West. He's wearing his trademark suit, and large, visible hearing aid, and he hollers off screen to his assistant to, "Get me Agent Chester Desmond out in Fargo, North Dakota." When the scene flicks back a step it's shown that he is almost nose-to-nose with a brunette in a grey dress and pearls, holding a notepad.

Cole is a man who shouts everything: mundane information and secrets alike. His lack of volume control might indicate a man without any finesse, but this is a misdirect. Because of his inability to choose the level of his tone, Cole resorts to codes and signs to impart his warnings and confidences.

The room is decorated in the quirky fashion of much of Lynch's films, with no care for verisimilitude. True to his artist's training, Lynch is more concerned with evoking a mood or establishing character through visual cues, lighting, and music. There are four lamps, of different sizes and styles, as if someone has raided a jumble sale. Two old-fashioned wooden filing cabinets, vestibules of information, flank Cole. An American flag stands meekly on the edge of the screen. This is barely America as we know it, and hardly the typical office of an important FBI officer, even in one of their regional offices.

Cole stands behind a bare desk, except for a telephone. A couple of black chairs, and waste paper cans sit nearby. His assistant leaves the room by exiting close to the camera, so her features are clear.

The subsequent cut is to a scene of chaos: a yellow school bus containing screaming children is parked on a grassy field. There are four FBI agents, all wearing classic brown raincoats over suits. One is patting down two men who are spread against the bus, another watches, while a third keeps his gun trained on the felons.

In the foreground Special Agent Chester 'Chet' Desmond (Chris Issak) handcuffs two blondes who are clearly coded as prostitutes. The tone is humorous, but the shrieking kids add an uneasy element to the bedlam. Chet is tall and handsome and goes about his business in a calm fashion.

A nearby car, with a flashing red light on top, buzzes and honks for attention. Chet leaves his job to another agent, and hurries to pick up the call coming through on the car phone. When Chet picks up the handset it's clear that he is wearing a ring on his right hand. This a small detail that is repeatedly shown throughout the subsequent scenes.[48]

---

[48] Cooper came to Twin Peaks also wearing a ring, which was used by the Giant to bring his attention to special events. It could be a shared symbol of brotherhood among certain agents that Cole has cherry picked. They wear their rings on their right hand, but the ring that brings fire, is worn on the left.

It's Cole, who bellows down the line that he's in Portland, Oregon. Continuing the light-hearted tone Chet winces and lowers the antenna on his car to reduce the strength of Cole's volume.

Cole says, "I've got a girl that's been murdered. Seventeen years old. Named Teresa Banks." Back in Cole's office, seen in the intercuts between Chet and Cole's conversation, a different woman gives Cole a blue mug of coffee.

She's blonde, with pearls, and dressed in a grey jacket and plum skirt. She also passes close to the camera so it is obvious she is not the first assistant Cole spoke to. It's not clear if this is just the woman in charge of coffee, or a transformation in the first assistant to indicate a destabilisation of reality. Due to the intercutting between Chet and Cole it's an easy detail is miss on first viewing, which would raise the suspicion of this being a subtle visual clue that reality is not going to proceed in a predictable fashion.

But the scene of abducted school children and surly hookers has already hinted at that. While not an extraordinary break with normal order, it establishes a farcical tone that skirts the bounds of everyday events.

Cole continues: "Chet I've got a surprise for you. Something interesting I would like to show you. Arrangements are being made, and I will meet you at the private Portland airport."

After a last shot of the school children, wailing with faces and hands pressed against the school bus windows, the next scene is slotted in effectively: an image of the cockpit of a single-prop plane, angling to land over picturesque countryside. With mountains, forests, and a lake in view, this is the landscape of *Twin Peaks*.

Chet climbs out of the hatch of the silver plane, carrying a battered leather suitcase. It's a scene that could have been shot in a hard-boiled 1930s detective film.

Waiting for him are Cole and Special Agent Sam Stanley (Kiefer Sutherland), in typical FBI suits and raincoats. Sam wears a dickie bow, and holds a bulky, bulbous, green case. Cole introduces him to Chet and suggests Chet give him "the glad hand", an old-fashioned term that solidifies Cole's connection to quaint mannerisms. It compounds the sense of these men being temporally disjointed.

"Sam's the man who cracked the Whitman case," Cole informs Chet. The two agents are polite, sizing each other up. When Cole states, "Chet, your surprise," he points toward a hanger where a single-prop, bright yellow plane is parked.

Almost under the wing, and a bright contrast, lurks a woman in a scarlet dress and matching wig (Kimberly Ann Cole). Most prominent is the blue rose attached to the top of her frock.

Chet appears unimpressed while Cole begins his coded speech: "Her name is Lil. She's my mother's sister's girl."

Lil scuttles forward, and scrunches up her highly made-up face as if smelling something disgusting. She spins in a circle, with one hand in her pocket, and her other hand opening and closing into a fist. The effect is akin to a clown or a mime.

Sam is bemused throughout most of the speech, and more so when Cole arcs his hand over his head so his fingers dangle like a grill over his features.

Chet is familiar with this game. "Federal," he states, and Cole nods.

Lil continues her antics, and Cole wishes them good luck before he tells Sam to, "stick with Chet. He's got his own M.O." There is no evidence of Dale Cooper so far, and the last statement seems like Cole's endorsement of the new agent in charge. As well as an indicator that Chet has a unique approach to solving crimes.

Cole heads back to the Philadelphia office, and the two agents get to know each other during a car ride.

Sam, standing in for the audience, doesn't understand the visual language of Cole's message, and asks Chet to decrypt it. Lil's "sour face" means local law enforcement will not cooperate with them, and "both eyes blinking means trouble higher up." The hand in the pocket is code for a hidden agenda, and the fist designates an aggressive attitude. Her walking in place means leg-work will be needed, and the relationship to Lil left out a reference to the uncle, which (along with the hand gesture) says there are issues with another bureau.

Chet probes Sam's skills by asking about Lil's dress, which Sam correctly noticed had been altered to fit her with black thread. "Tailored dresses are code for drugs," Chet says, while approving of Sam's observation. He asks if Sam noticed what was pinned to it.

At this point there is a close-up of the blue rose, which is clearly artificial; a 'natural' blue rose does not exist so this is a plain reminder of its impossibility. Since blue roses have been an object of fascination for many societies, it has long been used as a symbol in art and literature: often for immortality, perpetual love, or the unattainable. The blue rose is mystery incarnate, or in this case, manufactured (without genetic fiddling it can't be produced, and certainly wasn't naturally available in 1991 when *FWWM* was being shot).

To underscore the inexplicable quality of the blue rose, Chet adds, "But I can't tell you about that." Sam presses him, but Chet demurs. The blue rose represents wonder, and is not something that Sam, or we, can be told about yet. Knowledge of the blue rose is granted to the initiated through experience, not exposition.

Lil is a living cypher, a coded message not a person, and she presages how the detective process in *Twin Peaks*, and many criminal procedurals, breaks down the body of murdered women into clues. They exist as texts to be puzzled over and explained; mysteries in corporal form. It dangles the proposition that with the right attitude and dedication the enigma can be solved. But in *FWWM* the idea that typical sleuthing can penetrate extraordinary crimes is overturned. Dreadful transgressions can never be fully explained even with the assembly of all facts. The journey for answers catapults the seeker into the realm of emotion and pain, and language doesn't rule in that domain. It can never resolve the question: "why?" At best, it can offer the solution for "how?"

Chet's tutoring ends. From now on the audience is expected to generate its own sense.

In an interesting piece of cut dialogue from the script Sam queries why this wasn't imparted directly, and Chet says of Cole: "He talks loud. And he loves his code." Since Lynch is playing Cole, this seems a clear indicator that we must seek a different set of correspondences to access the full narrative. It also demonstrates that Lynch above all will cut 'on the nose' explanations. Cole's deafness and predilection for code can be understood from watching the movie and paying attention: they don't require articulation.

The first stop for the agents is local law enforcement: Deer Meadow's Sheriff's Department—its outdoor sign has antlers hanging above it, pointing out, and suggestive of attack. Inside, Chet is hunched over at the counter, clearly impatient, while Sam sits primly on a sofa, looking about in an inquisitive fashion. The seated receptionist (Elizabeth McCarthy) ignores Chet, reading a magazine and chewing gum. A stuffed stag's head hangs on the wall, and the light is diffused by slatted blinds on the windows. The room seems stuffy. Most egregious: there is an empty pot of coffee close to Sam. There is no hospitality available. This is the antithesis of the generosity of food and spirit available in the Twin Peaks Sheriff's Department.

A rack of guns hangs behind the secretary, and Chet fidgets.

Tall, moustachioed Deputy Cliff Howard (Rick Aiello) saunters out, radiating the contempt of a heel. He doesn't introduce himself, leaving it to Chet to speak first. The agent's request to see Sheriff Cable is met with a snort, and snickers from the receptionist. The Deputy instructs Chet to take a seat by Sam, "because it's going to be a while." The Deer Meadow duo break into laughter, and he leans close to her so they collude in their joint derision.

After a couple of other quips, Chet loses patience. "I've enough of the waiting room now," he says and moves behind the counter. The deputy immediately blocks his way. There is a stand-off for a moment, with Chet holding up his hand as if he's going to back off, but it's a commanding move that stops the deputy in his tracks.

In a swift and surprising attack Chet grabs the deputy by the nose and uses it to control the man, while the secretary gawks. He forces the deputy down into the corner, and snaps his hand off the deputy's nose, causing the lawman intense pain. Chet has demonstrated his "unique M.O.", and under his laconic manner lies an impatient man of action.

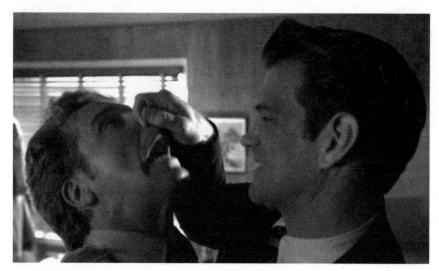

It's often implied in critiques of *FWWM* that Chet is a simple stand-in for Agent Dale Cooper, since this section was originally envisioned for Cooper, but that ignores the agents' different characteristics and nuances, and Isaak's tidy bit of acting. It also forgets that Lynch adapts to actors on the set and encourages them to fill out their roles. The first draft of the opening of the film may have been intended for MacLachlan, but by the shooting of the film Lynch had adjusted his intentions, and Isaak put his stamp upon the role. Engels has commented on this:

> *Chet Desmond was born from Kyle's reticence to be in the movie. Then we re-thought who this person was and it became a full-blown person who we thought was pretty cool. Chet, from Chet Baker; and Desmond from Norma Desmond—it's a noirname. Both David and I love Chet Baker. But all these things work as a plus. Now we had two agents and to use a musician [Chris Isaak] was pretty cool.*[49]

After an instruction to the secretary to start a fresh pot of coffee, Chet strolls into the back office. Sheriff Cable (Gary Bullock) is a balding hostile man, seated behind his desk. A huge steel saw hangs on his wall—in the establishing shot it seems like a set of iron teeth emerging in a line

---

[49] Thorne, *The Essential Wrapped in Plastic*, Kindle edition, location 5833.

from Cable's head toward Chet. It could be something out of one of Lynch's early surrealist short films.

Chet speaks over Cable's first angry questions, but the sheriff is not easily intimidated. Their interaction is antagonistic, and mostly shot from the level of Cable's seated height, so Chet looms over him. But Cable does not rise to stand. Chet barely holds himself in check, and Cable threatens him directly.

When Cable surrenders the Teresa Banks files, he speaks about the dead woman as if she was one of the deer decorating his office: "A basic kill. Banks was a drifter and nobody knew her." Chet gets directions to their morgue out back, and makes it clear that he and Sam will stay as long as it takes to finish their examination.

On the way out Chet spots an old black and white photo of the sheriff, holding a long, bent iron bar over his head. 'CABLE BENDS STEEL' reads the caption. Chet gives the sheriff a reassessing stare, and then heads out with Sam to examine the body of the murdered woman.

CABLE BENDS STEEL

Cable and his Deputy share a meaningful look after the interlopers leave their domain. They are unhappy with the intrusion.

The door to the morgue is a rustic wooden affair, as if it leads into a barn. Sam makes an irrelevant observation as Chet opens the door that "...I figure this whole office, furniture included, is worth 27,000 dollars."

It is something an accountant would say, not a forensics expert, and Chet has no comment. This assessment of the value of objects is something Sam continues to do in several other scenes in the original screenplay, which aren't present in the film. It's not a strange tic, but a part of Sam's character. He is obtuse when it comes to living people, but a whiz at evaluating objects or examining the dead.

Mentions of Teresa Banks and her murder were peppered throughout the early episodes of *Twin Peaks*, but there was little known about her, other than a few details. This first image of her in the film is uniformly mournful. She lies on the metal body tray, her head tilted back, and her mouth open as if expressing surprise. Her eyelids are slightly open and her eyes are downcast. Her peroxide blonde hair is roughly cut and stiff.

Most tellingly, her entire body is coated in a film of soot, as if she was suffocated by a smoking blaze. Teresa has walked through fire, and it has extinguished her spirit.

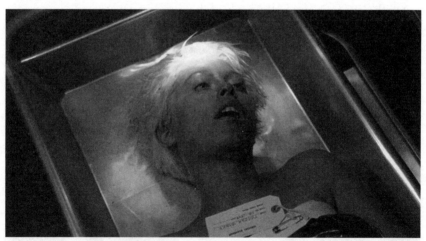

A paper tag with her name on is attached to a large metal safety pin, and is her only remaining identifier.

This is a haunting image of Teresa, a lonely, forgotten woman who has been brutalised and jettisoned. It's the first example of a profound readjustment in emphasis from the TV series, which was about the trappings of investigation of victims who were fetishised as trophies, by their killer and those who kept their remaining items. Banks and Laura Palmer in

Twin Peaks were a collection of evidence. In *FWWM* they are shown as real people with complicated lives, and their deaths are a tragedy and a crime.

The small, cramped morgue where the two men work with the body has the trappings of a recommissioned tool shed. The two-doored mortuary refrigerator looks more like an oven—its outside is even streaked with soot. It is the setting for a fairy tale rather than a forensic examination.

Chet reads Teresa's file out loud, slowly and with empathy for the dead girl, while Sam pulls on gloves happily with a desire to get down to business.

The tally of small details about her life—her temporary residence at the Fat Trout Trailer Park and her night shift job at Hap's Diner—are scant with truly personal information. When Chet says, "No one came to claim her body," it cuts to a close-up of Teresa's face, which seems aghast at her abandonment.

As he adds, "No known next of kin," the film cuts to a close-up of her eye, looking at the audience directly. It could be considered an accusation, or the mere acknowledgement to the viewer that she existed. It then cuts to a close-up of her mouth, open as if to say something, but forever silenced by her killer. Sam may be eagerly professional when dealing with the minutiae of evidence, but both men treat Teresa's body with care. It's an obvious contrast to the indifference and hostility of those who have left her like an animal trophy awaiting a quick disposal (a giant metal hook, like those used to display carcasses, hangs above her).

Sam begins recording his observations. He gently takes her head in both hands, and moves it from side to side. There is an eerie quality to this handling of the body, as her face is moved to look directly at the camera. She seems ready to protest.

At the same time Sam catalogues the dreadful injuries that resulted in her death: "Crushed skull. Probable cause: repeated blows to the back of the head by a blunt, obtuse-angled object." There is no need for any flashback to the opening scene. The echo of her screams and the wet sound of the death blow linger in the recent memory.

Sam steps back, and gets an overview. "I wonder where her ring is?" He says, and we see her blackened hand, with a clear band where the ring used to be. Her fingernails are painted red—always a warning sign in Lynchian language—and strangely scratched.

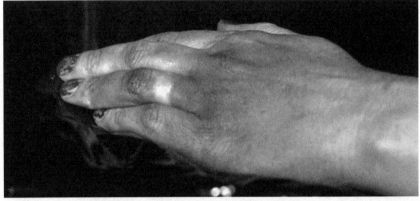

Chet checks the personal effects but there is no ring.

Sam spots a problem with the ring finger of the left hand and pulls over his special machine to check it. The music winds up in a weird disharmony to increase the discomfort as the nail is pealed back from the skin with a sickening crack. A piece of paper is discovered with the letter T printed on it. Her body has been branded by the killer.[50] She is also a text to be figured out.

---

[50] It is explained in *Twin Peaks* that the letters would have eventually spelled out ROBERT, BOB's name.

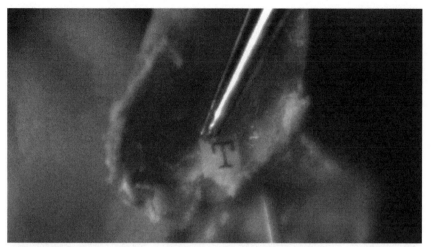

The two men examine their find, and turn their gaze to the dead woman, puzzled. The film cuts to a tight shot of her face: her mouth is open but she cannot answer their questions.

The music spools down into a discordant squawk and it fades to black.

It returns as the agents lock up the morgue at 3.30 am in the morning. They decide to go to Hap's for a very early breakfast.

In the establishing shot 'Hap's' is a blue neon sign stark against a pitch-black moonless sky, but it's the half burned-out neon, crying clown that's the disturbing element; almost an echo of Lil's face. A couple of cars are pulled up front, and it quickly cuts to the middle of a conversation with an old, grizzled man dressed in shades of black. It's in a dingy back room, with a flickering light that indicates an unstable energy. The printed badge on his chest reads 'SAY HELLO TO JACK' but the HELLO has been crossed out, and GOODBYE scrawled above it. This is not a friendly guy.

Jack (C.H. Evans) advises the agents to speak to the waitress. "Now Irene is her name and it is night. Don't go any further with it." In the room with Jack are a bearded older man, and a man in dark glasses working on a light fixture which is throwing up sparks.

The main room of the diner is typical Americana: red leather round stools, a rectangular pink counter, and utterly abandoned in the dead of night except for one couple and Irene. In the corner, through the doorway, the flicking light continues, with the buzz of electricity. Red shadows of neon signs are splashed over a wall. It has a half-life existence, barely animated: a place where secrets and odd characters congregate.

The two agents sit and talk to Irene (Sandra Kinder), perhaps the truest depiction of a jaded, middle-aged night-shift waitress that has ever graced the screen.

She serves them coffee as they make introductions, her cigarette drooping disapprovingly from her lips. Her dowdy brown cardigan covers up most of her lollipop pink uniform.

Irene drawls her description of her co-worker: "She only worked here a month. Nice Girl. She never seemed to get here on time though. If you ask me, she had a little problem with..." and she sniffs dramatically to indicate cocaine. Nothing would ever surprise this woman.

When she admits she never saw Teresa take drugs, Chet needles her a little about if she's ever used drugs. She becomes indignant, and more so when pedantic Sam can't help pointing out that nicotine and caffeine are drugs. "Those drugs are legal!" she glares at Sam, incensed by his stupidity.

Chet is unimpressed by her assessment of Teresa's death as a "freak accident", and he drops the line of inquiry. Down the counter a man in a plaid shirt (G. Kenneth Davidson), sitting with a chic French woman in black (Paige Bennet), perks up. "Are you asking about that little girl that got murdered?" the man asks.

But he claims not to know "shit from Shinola" when Chet presses him for information. Sam wonders if they should question him further and Chet darts an amazed look at his partner. Sam might be super at forensics, but he continues to demonstrate no ability to figure out people. Chet notices that Sam is holding the handle of his coffee cup, and impishly asks him for the time. Sam obligingly turns his wrist to find out and spills the coffee upon himself.

Chet laughs, but acts kind of sorry as well. It's very early in the morning and they are frayed. Irene returns with a titbit: "Once, for about three days, just before her time, Teresa's arm went completely dead." She reveals it was her left arm that went numb—the ring-bearing arm. Sam suggests he would need to bring the body to Portland to examine the arm for nerve damage, and Chet concurs. There is an impression that he would prefer to proceed without Sam.

The man in plaid reiterates his first question, and the woman beside him pats his shoulder, as if used to dealing with this loop. He is a record, stuck on repeat. Chet and Sam ignore the man as if he never spoke.

In a twilight location such as Hap's Diner, people have only an echoed existence. This also implies that the diner could be another one of the staging areas for the otherworldly entities who will break into the film so vividly in a short while. It's the bleak, damaged replica of the Double R Diner, the vital hub of Twin Peaks social life. This town is the flipside of Twin Peaks, and displays its darkness willingly.

One of the 'missing pieces' that was shot but excised from *FWWM*, happens in the car park after this scene. It's a telling exchange of dialogue, and probably cut because it hindered the pace and didn't add to the movie.

Chet suggests, "Sam, I think you and I aughta see the sun rise at the Fat Trout Trailer Park." After a long night and peculiar conversations Sam seems unable to figure out if Chet is being serious. "Agent Desmond, are you talking to me in code?" he asks.

Chet replies, "No, Sam, I'm speaking plainly and I mean exactly what I said."

It strikes me that this could be the typical conversation that David Lynch encounters with fans of his work: a confusion over what is 'real' and what is 'untrue' in his films. Yet the obvious answer is that all cinema, all fiction, is a lie. Even our personal narratives can be the biggest fiction we tell daily.

In Lynch's films what is perceived as scrambled is no doubt plain-speaking to him.

III

The Fat Trout Trailer Park is one of many named locations with a familiar resonance that populate Lynch's films. It's one of his liminal spaces: a 'stuck' place for transitory people. Trailers have the potential to be mobile, and transported to another location, but they almost never move. There is an inherent contradiction in the purpose of the park.

The sign that proclaims the trailer park depicts a large trout leaping out of the river, its mouth open, gasping. It is a fish out of water, literally, a creature caught moving from its natural realm through an alien environment, taking a leap of faith hoping it will splash back to its home. But in that moment in the sign, the trout is suspended; frozen. Teresa's mouth was agape in a similar manner in the morgue.

This park can be a place of transit from one place to another, or one state to another, but not via normal means, and it brings inherent risk.

Chet and Sam arrive early in the morning at the trailer park — a rooster crows as they approach the home of the manager, Carl Rodd (Harry Dean Stanton). Scrawled with marker on the rough door is the warning: "DO NOT EVER DISTURB BEFORE 9 AM . . . EVER".

Hand-written notes on scraps of paper and cardboard from his tenants are thumb-tacked to his door: 'Rod, My cat is gone, Millie'; 'Rod, My fridge does not stay cold, Larry'; 'Rod, I'm moving out, Sam'; 'Rod, something's wrong with your trailer'; 'Rod, the hole in my roof is getting bigger'; 'Rod, my trailer has a leak, fix it by tomorrow'. This is a man with a plethora of problems who doesn't seem in a hurry to solve any of them. And the homes in the Fat Trout Trailer Park are in a perpetual state of decay.

The agents only notice the directive on the door after Chet pounds on it, and wakes the grumpy manager. Carl is shouting abuse before he opens

up. The men scramble to have their IDs ready so they can placate Carl when he appears. He's resentful of having to take another group of people on the tour of the crime scene. "That goddam trailer is more popular than uncle's day at a whorehouse." Wearing his plaid robe over shirt and jeans he escorts them to the trailer.

The interior of Teresa's trailer is typical: cheap wood panelling that would be freezing in winter, tacky pictures probably hung by a previous occupant, a small stove and a commonplace kettle. She hangs her bras on a wire drying rack, close to the electric outlet. A sink, hotplate, coffee pot, microwave, and spice rack comprise the kitchen. Net curtains filter the sunlight.

The men stand in the middle of the tiny space and survey the loneliness of Teresa's life. From just outside on the littered porch Carl shouts: "Everything's exactly as she left it. I haven't touched a god damn thing."

The scene dissolves to a close-up of a photograph and the scarlet lips of a woman. It's Teresa Banks when she was alive. This is radically different from the previous close-up of her dead, protesting mouth. Here she is alive, and with that red lippy, she's a vibrant siren. The music becomes a little discordant, and Chet scrutinises the picture, attempting to get a fix on the woman he's investigating.

When he urges Sam over to examine the image, the full-sized photo-graph of Teresa is revealed: wearing a simple outfit of a white t-shirt and jeans, her arms crossed, cigarette in hand, directly looking to camera with a challenging gaze. The photo is affixed to the fridge by a cat magnet; the twee element adds a contrast to her image as the confident seductress. The photo appears to have a scorch mark or damage on the right-hand side of her head. As if she was already attracting fire.

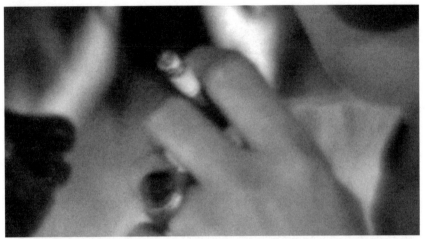

Most importantly, she's wearing the ring which was missing at the autopsy: it's got a gold band with a green stone and a carving in it. She appears comfortable with the ring, as if proud of it.

Carl sloops off to make coffee, while Chet remains staring at Teresa: her lips and captivating eyes. He seems half in love with her, a spell cast from the past. When Carl returns with three cups of strong Joe, the men are grateful: until they taste it. "This stuff's got the sting of the 48 hour blend," says Chet as Sam coughs.

The men chuckle in shared bonhomie, and Sam, eager to be included says: "We sure do need a bit of a wake-up Agent Desmond, don't we?" Chet doesn't respond, as if there is nothing he can say to this, and Sam repeats himself. Chet laughs, and agrees, but the exchange underscores that they are a mis-matched pair who are not in synch, and that Chet might still be dazed from Teresa's stare and the terrible coffee.

The next shot begins outside, and moves smoothly along with the sound of wind until it enters the doorway. The unsettling music plays and the camera switches to reveal an old, petite, hunched woman hobbling with a cane (she is referred to in the credits as the 'curious woman'—Ingrid Brucato). She has an icepack over her right eye, as if she has sustained a recent injury, but most importantly, her face is coated in soot.

She peers in at the men, and Carl is thunderstruck by her.

When Chet asks if she knew Teresa Banks she trembles with fear, shakes her head, and slowly backs out of the room. She has witnessed something dreadful and can't speak of it. Carl is frozen in place; her countenance has triggered a memory.

It cuts to the image of an electricity pole in the trailer park, that's numbered '324810', and underneath it is a large '6'.[51] There's the sound that could be someone making a whooping sound (which is later demonstrated by the Man From Another Space). There is no explanation for this image or if the numbers are important, but what it probably implies it that Carl has been swept up in a current, which erratically pulses through this location. His reverie breaks, but he remains upset.

"You see, I've already gone places," he confesses. "I just want to say where I am." In the stasis of the trailer park Carl can escape his past, but

---

[51] Lynch has repeatedly said that he considers some numbers, and combination of numbers—such as on licence plates—to be lucky. These numbers add up to 18, which when added again make 9. 9 is an upside down 6. The charm is that you can make any sense you wish out of it. It appears significant, therefore it becomes so.

he does not want to go to the weird places again, even when they beckon.

The next intercut scene is of mountains and trees, and the wind swaying the firs' branches. It's the first *Twin Peaks*-like intercut, and it carries with it the strangeness of the curious woman and her odd effect upon Carl. The mystery is deepening...

The agents return to the Deer Meadow Sheriff's Department, and Sam has his truck ready to transport Teresa's body. Of course, there's a stand-off with Cable and his sidekick Cliff. "You're not taking that body anywhere," Cable states at first.

Chet is direct. "We're taking the body back to Portland. There's not a thing you can do about it." He asks about the missing ring, and Cable makes a cheap joke about the telephone.

In the 'missing pieces' and in the script, there is a fight between Chet and Cable at this point, which demonstrates Cable's considerable prowess, but also that Chet is a talented pugilist. The special agent wins the bout, and claims the body. He has become Teresa's champion, despite her death.

Sam prepares to leave for Portland and Chet says he's going back to the trailer park. At this point Sam raises the Blue Rose again, and its image is shown on the screen for a moment.

"You're going back to the trailer park for the Blue Rose."

Chet does not gainsay him. It's implied that both Gordon Cole and Chet are aware of another matter at work in this murder, and one they have encountered before. It can't be explained to Sam, because Sam is a numbers man, without intuition. The people in *Twin Peaks* who are pulled into other realms are those who are sensitive and receptive to different possibilities. Sam counts the cost of everything but doesn't know their value. It's unlikely that Chet could explain the Blue Rose to Sam, even if he tried.

Perhaps this pairing between the men was a test of Sam's ability to be privy to a Blue Rose case—if so he failed. In the pilot episode of *Twin Peaks*, Agent Cooper instructs his assistant Diane to assign Special Agent Albert Rosenfeld (Miguel Ferrer) to Laura Palmer's autopsy, not Sam. Word has got out that Sam's not the man if you've got a case that requires sensitivity.[52]

The image of the blue rose pinned to the scarlet dress dissolves slowly into the image of the Fat Trout Trailer Park. It's dusk, an in-between time. Carl escorts Chet around, in between rows of trailers. An electricity pole is centre in the screen, cutting it in half. Carl points out Deputy Cliff's trailer, and his red truck (of course it's red, a signal for danger) parked next to it.

Carl is dragged away by a demanding tenant, and Chet glances up the pole at the crossing of wires that cut through the park—a transport of energy. It's also a crossroads of sort, which traditionally is a place where occult powers can conjure up entities.

As he looks down it's clear that this is the same electricity pole that triggered Carl's earlier fugue state. And perhaps this is the only significance of the numbers on the pole—so it's clear that this is the location that prompted Carl's introspection. A centre point between Cliff and Teresa's homes, but connected via an unseen link. The low, eerie sound of yodelling seeps under the music again.

Chet turns in the direction directly opposite Cliff's trailer. Behind him Cliff's trailer would be in the 6 o'clock position, and Teresa's would be at the 9 o'clock position, which would make the trailer directly facing him at twelve o'clock.

---

[52] In one of the excised scenes from *FWWM* Cooper interrogates Sam about Chet's disappearance, and Cooper clearly finds him tiresome.

This trailer is smaller with a set of wheels, set on concrete blocks, and more likely to be moved to another location. It's lit up like a beacon, and has red curtains—always a sign of otherworldly interactions—hanging mid-way in the windows. Chet drifts toward it as if pulled by a magnet, and the thrumming score of deep strings is like the sound of electricity through wires.

Chet approaches the trailer, knocks on the door, and peers in the window. Something brings his attention to the wheel, and underneath the trailer.

The summoning mound of earth has been created, and on top, is Teresa's ring. This time it is very clear: a thick gold band, set with an oval green stone, and etched into it with black lines is the Owl glyph first seen in the Owl Cave in *Twin Peaks*.[53]

Chet reaches for it with his right hand, his own ring gleaming, and the image freezes, then fades to black.

---

[53] The ring is commonly referred to as the Owl Cave Ring.

IV

The next section begins with the shadow of the Liberty Bell, and the title: 'PHILADELPHIA'. This is the birthplace of American freedom, but crucially for this film, the birthplace of Lynch's career as an artist and filmmaker. The Liberty Bell also cannot peal: its true function is broken. It cannot raise an alarm or signal a celebration. It is an object that works only in the abstract realm of ideas.

The camera moves up to show the cracked liberty bell[54], before segueing into a huge office space with Special Agent Dale Cooper making an entrance.

He walks past a framed black and white etching of the Liberty Bell, which hangs on a column. It's an incongruous detail, implying a micro-universe inside the larger world has been created.[55] Cooper approaches Gordon, who's sitting behind a desk. Cooper squats in front of Cole, and says, "Gordon, it's 10:10 am on February 16th."

His boss checks his watch, unsure, but says nothing waiting for Cooper to elaborate. "I was worried about today because of the dream I told you about." Gordon shoots Cooper an enigmatic look.

The following scenes could be Cooper's dream. If so it is not well signalled. What is 'real' is deliberately left vague. The next sequence contains some of the most ambiguous elements in the film and works as a deliberately disorientating effect upon the viewer.

---

[54] The bell was cast with the phrase: 'Proclaim LIBERTY Throughout all the Land unto all the Inhabitants Thereof'.

[55] It's also evocative of surrealist Belgian painter René Magritte's famous *The Treachery of Images*. This poor replica of the Liberty Bell is obviously fake, yet the previous image of the bell is not 'real' either. All reside in the dream of film, and are mere representations of higher concepts, situated to spark deeper meditation.

Cooper enters a long, bland corridor with a blue carpet[56], and stands in front of a video camera hanging from the roof. He stands still, staring squarely at it.

It cuts to a black and white image of Cooper on a TV screen, and back to Cooper in the hallway, before he walks into a nearby room. A security officer is sitting in the room observing the monitor—it's the middle of three screens. One is shows an image of an entrance, and the other of another corridor. The image on the middle screen matches Cooper's actions.

Cooper repeats this sequence, and returns to the security man's office to check the screen—which shows an empty corridor. At this point the film cuts to a scene of a blue elevator door opening with the number '7' beside it.

Cooper re-emerges from the office to stand in front of the security camera. From the elevator strides a tanned Special Agent Philip Jeffries (David Bowie), wearing a light linen suit, a garish shirt, and red shoes. He looks like someone who should be in South America, not a FBI Bureau office in Philadelphia.

---

[56] Lynch had requested that the colour blue not appear in the palette of *Twin Peaks* (Duke, *Reflections*, location 3801). It's a cool tone, which suggests skies, and slow movement.

Before *FWWM* Lynch made **Wild at Heart**, which contained an allegory of **The Wizard of Oz**. It's as if Jeffries is Dorothy, displaced from another universe, but back in 'Texas' for a brief visit.

Jeffries walks behind Cooper, who doesn't notice. Cooper dashes back into the security office to observe his image, which eerily remains fixed on the screen, temporally frozen, as Jeffries moves past him. The impression is that Jeffries' presence is causing a disruption to causal reality.

Cooper shouts for Gordon, and sprints after Jeffries.

Gordon immediately recognises Jeffries when he enters the room, and it's revealed that Albert is seated behind a different desk in the cavernous room. As the landscape of this room, with its cooling blue carpet, is made clear, it's obvious that realism has been abandoned. Forensics experts don't sit in the same giant room as the Regional Director.

Cooper hurries in after Jeffries, and Gordon shouts: "Cooper, meet the long-lost Philip Jeffries, you may have heard of him from the Academy." It establishes that Jeffries has been absent, and has a reputation.

Jeffries acts agitated, and with a southern accent, says, "Well now, I'm not going to talk about Judy, in fact we're not going to talk about Judy at all, we're going to keep her out of it."[57] This nonsense talk also points to the inability of language to articulate the strangeness he has witnessed and the spaces he has travelled. Jeffries is a Cassandra: doomed to speak prophecies no one can understand.

Judy is one of the most discussed mysteries of *FWWM* and generates a great deal of debate. This series of scenes was originally envisioned differently in the script: they are meant to be intercut with the introduction of Laura Palmer as well as showing the location from which Jeffries has just shifted through time and space. While some of these scenes are now available as part of the 'missing pieces' extras on the 2014 Blu-ray boxed set, they mainly serve to tantalise about the greater plan that Lynch and Engels had in mind.

The technical difficulty is that the long scene in which Jeffries delivers his disjointed speech opens with the line about Judy, therefore making it impossible to excise all reference to the character when the film was

---

[57] Judy Garland played Dorothy in *The Wizard of Oz*, a woman who travelled to another reality populated by strange characters, and returns home (temporarily).

reduced to its final form. This is a good example of how the demands of the filmmaking process—the long evolution from script to shoot to editing room—can profoundly affect the completed story. In the final version of *FWWM*, Judy is a ghostly imprint of a bigger narrative.[58] Rather than ignore her completely, there is one further reference to her later, and it drives fans' fascination with the character.

As with most of Lynch's more difficult films, the larger story is teased but an interposing veil prevents us from seeing its entire body.

Since this section could be construed as a warning dream Cooper experienced previously, the breakdown in time in space is typical of the instability of dreams.

When Jeffries points at Cooper and asks: "Who do you think that is there?", there is a strong possibility that he is seeing or foretelling Cooper's doppelgänger—which is from a future event.[59]

At Jeffries' denunciation of Cooper the scene is overlaid with blue static. The image of a red-suited figure wearing a white mask with a long pointed nose, and holding a stick, surfaces—this is a character known in the credits as the Jumping Man (Carlton Lee Russell).[60] It fades in and out, distorting the conversation that is taking place in the room.

The effect is of an interrupting signal, one that is gleefully stirring things up, confusing Jeffries further, and distorting the audience's understanding of what is happening. Upon first viewing this part of the film wrenches expectations sideways. There have been odd elements so far, but this is outright invasion.

Time and space distorts and warps.

---

[58] The best understanding based on what is available is that Jeffries found the Owl Cave Ring at Judy's in Seattle, and the artefact projected him into one of the meetings of the otherworldly entities above the convenience store. It's likely that the same has occurred to Agent Desmond, but it's not clear why Jeffries seems to retain some ability to move through space/time again. The ring acts differently upon people, depending on their reasons for taking/accepting it. It possesses tremendous transformative power.

[59] Jeffries appears to have moved forward in time (in a deleted scene he appears shocked to discover it's February 1989).

[60] Russell recollects that Lynch told him during his one day of shooting, that he was "this talisman come to life." *Moving Through Time: Fire Walk With Me Memories* (Special Feature in the *Twin Peaks* Blu Ray box set).

Albert's amused comment, "Suffered some bumps on the old noggin, eh Phil?", and Gordon's declaration of Cooper's identity fade out as the Jumping Man jitters while he casts his spell. His reality overrides the world of detectives, and the otherworldly parallel realm, known as 'above the convenience store', snaps into view.

It's not clear if Jeffries voluntarily broke through time and space to deliver a warning, or has been projected due to an accidental use of power, but the interruption has given the entities a chance to materialise to the audience.[61]

The FBI agents in the room are oblivious to this extra dimension, except perhaps for Jeffries. This display is for the viewer, to indicate the actions of a different collection of agents. They are the double of the FBI Bureau: a group of affiliated entities who have an interest in people and events in our realm.

The Jumping Man's spellcasting works and he solidifies into view. He is not wearing a mask as it first appeared: his face *is* the mask, as if one he wore has merged with his face. His red suit, shirt, and tie are different shades of red.

---

[61] The screenplay, and extra filmed scenes, indicate that Jeffries has been in Buenos Aires at one point before this disruption, but the time period is unclear. Once Jeffries entered the other space, notions of normal chain of events cease to be straightforward.

His job done, the jumping man retreats to his soapbox, and the full view of room above the convenience store is revealed. The first establishing shot is high up, looking down. The room has three windows, and light seeps in through random holes scraped in the dirty, desiccated paper that covers them. The walls and floor are filthy.

Foregrounded are the Man From Another Place and BOB sitting opposite each other with a green Formica table between them. There are four bowls on the table of various sizes, and all of them are filled with creamed corn. There is an impression that they are peers, if not friendly, and distinct from the onlookers.

Sitting in a row, observing them, from left to right are: The Electrician (Calvin Lockhart), Mrs. Tremond (Frances Bay), Mrs. Tremond's grandson (Jonathan J. Leppell), the Second Woodsman (David Brisbin), and the Woodsman (Jürgen Prochnow).

Of this motley assortment of characters only Mrs. Tremond and her grandson have been seen before: in episode 9 of *Twin Peaks*, 'Coma', when Donna takes over Laura's Meals on Wheels route.[62] In that instance, Mrs. Tremond directed Donna toward her next-door-neighbour, Harold Smith (Lenny Von Dohlen), the agoraphobic man Laura befriended. When

---

[62] One of the season two episodes of *Twin Peaks* directed by Lynch, and in that episode the grandson was played by Austin Jack Lynch, his son.

Donna returns to the duo's house some days later it is denied that they even lived there—a different Mrs. Tremond is resident.[63] Donna's discovery of Harold, and the existence of Laura's secret diary, directly lead to Harold's suicide.[64]

As will become obvious later, Mrs. Tremond and her grandson are lower grade entities, pushing people along to suit the interests of the more powerful Man From Another Place and BOB. The grandson may even be an apprentice, with the opportunity to level up later depending on the success of his and his guardian grandmother's prompts. In the 'Coma' episode he was described as a magician in training, and performed a trick by transporting creamed corn from a dish into his hands.

As is usual in these Lynchian other spaces, the creatures that abide there have been filmed in reverse and then played forwards to give their actions and oblique remarks an even stranger quality. Fire gouts, and the Woodsman seems to reach to adjust a huge machine as the signal destabilises slightly. It takes effort to broadcast this scene.

"Garmonbozia" the Man From Another Place says, and it cuts to a close-up of the creamed corn. He proclaims "This is a Formica table." and "Green is its color."[65] while he rubs his hands over the surface. In this weird realm simple facts are not taken for granted, and need to be reiterated.

The static returns and Jeffries is heard telling the agents in the other reality: "It was a dream, we live inside a dream."[66]

In the meeting room Mrs. Tremond looks down at her grandson.

---

[63] It indicates that the Tremonds merely take the name of the previous inhabitant, as they do with Chalfont at the Fat Trout Trailer Park. Their 'real' identity is never known.

[64] *"J'ai une âme solitaire"* reads his suicide note, which Cooper translates as "I am a lonely soul"—the same words spoken by the grandson when Donna first meets them. There is an implication that old lady and her grandson could be partly responsible for Harold's death. Or it is another proof of the child's ability: he predicts Harold's last words.

[65] There is a hole dug out of the Formica surface, which *might* be the green oval set into the Owl Cave Ring, but the material doesn't quite match.

[66] In Lynch's book, *Catching the Big Fish: Meditation, Consciousness, and Creativity* (New York: Penguin, 2006), p. 139, he includes a quote from the *Aitareya Upanishad*: "We are like the spider. We weave our life and then move along in it. We are like the dreamer who dreams and then lives in the dream. This is true for the entire universe."

Slumped in his seat he points at BOB and says "Fell a victim". This could be interpreted as an instruction to BOB to strike again.

The Man From Another Place states "With this ring, I thee wed." which indicates that the ring establishes a connection to one of the possessing spirits. Underneath, Jefferies moans, "The ring, the ring," and the Man From Another Place laughs.

The Woodsman slaps his knee, and there is an extreme close-up in the mouth of the Jumping Man as he regurgitates the word, "Electricity".

The wide shot of the room returns, as Jeffries says "Listen up and listen carefully. I've been to one of their meetings."

The Jumping Man returns to his podium, and the red curtains fade in over a corner of the room. Time and space is changing again.

The grandson is seen holding a white mask with a long pointed nose in front of his face, which is similar to the Jumping Man's, except it doesn't have eyes or a mouth. Instead a stick pokes out of its forehead. This is like a proto-version of the Jumping Man, as if the grandson may one day evolve into a creature like the Jumping Man if he practices hard enough.[67]

---

[67] In *Twin Peaks*, Audrey Horne (Sherilyn Fenn) resorts to covering her face with a white mask when concealing her identity from her father, who believes she is the new prostitute in his stable of girls at One Eyed Jacks. It was innocence trying to shield itself from a predator, where here, the young child's face of innocence is not to be trusted. Underneath his 'mask' is something older and more knowing.

The grandson uncovers his young face as Jeffries shouts "I found something!", then places the mask over his face again.

The camera moves in tight to the mask where the eyes should be, and when it is coyly moved to one side this time it reveals a monkey's face.[68] Jefferies says, "Then there they were." A primal creature is hidden behind the façade. The mask slips back into place, and BOB—crouched over—and the Man From Another Place walk over a corner of zig-zag floor and leave via a parting in the red curtains.

Once they depart the meeting room, the static returns, the signal loses cohesion, and Jeffries face is overlaid, screaming. This is him returning to his previous location.

In between blasts of static, Jeffries is shown speaking and gesturing to the agents, before a wild swinging shot of electricity wires and Gordon yelling, "He's gone, he's gone!" The connection has been lost.

The static abates: an empty chair remains. "Albert, call the front desk," Gordon yells.

The world of detectives re-asserts itself, and rationality attempts to kick back in, but explanations are not forthcoming.

"I've got the front desk now, he was never here." Albert continues, "And news from Deer Meadow: Agent Chester Desmond had disappeared."

"Gordon, what's going on?" implores Cooper.

The men try to resort to evidentiary standards, and examine the video tape from earlier. Jeffries is visible behind the out-of-synch image of Cooper. They know Jeffries has visited—and the front door was not his point of entry or departure. Yet no comment is made on the fact that Cooper's image should be an impossibility. There is no longer a reference point for reality.

"But where did he go?" asks Gordon as they stare at the screen showing two FBI agents out of time. "And where is Chester Desmond?"

The story jumps to the Fat Trout Trailer Park, and Carl points out Teresa Banks' trailer to Agent Cooper, while repeating the same informa-

---

[68] The monkey never appeared in the script. It was something Lynch devised during the shoot. First Assistant Director Deepak Nayar noted, "These are things he would tell me a couple of days before. 'And have a monkey ready.' He tells you not knowing exactly when, but basically have them ready." *Moving Through Time: Fire Walk With Me Memories.*

tion he told Chet. A dilapidated white picket fence guards the front of trailer 19, Teresa's home, with a blue dingy band around the outside, and its rickety porch slapped on the side.

Carl recounts his actions, and that he didn't see Chet again after he left the FBI agent. Cooper apologizes for waking him, and Carl says "I was having a bad dream anyway." As if he has also seen the vision recently offered to the viewer. But it's unlikely that anyone in the Fat Trout Trailer Park gets much rest. Like Chet, the instinctive Cooper immediately gravitates away from Deputy Cliff's trailer, much to Carl's exasperation. "God damn these people are confusing," he mutters (a sentiment many can agree with).

But the trailer that intrigued Agent Desmond has vanished, and all that remains is disturbed earth, and perhaps scorch marks. Cooper asks who owned it, and Carl replies that it was an old woman and her grandson, but he says their name is Charlfont, and it was also the name of the people who rented the pace before. The 'Tremonds' have been at their identity theft again.

Chet's car remains parked at the trailer park. A film of dirt lies over it, as if a sand storm blew over, or it's been abandoned for weeks. Written in lurid pink is 'Let's Rock', an expression used by the Man from Another Place in *Twin Peaks*.

The last camera shot is from inside the car, and through the layer of pink paint as if some invisible person is seated in the car, sizing up Cooper.

It cuts to the river, and the agent reporting via tape recorder to Diane. Cooper has no leads, but a bad feeling based on the crime scenario that the killer may strike again. His face is in full sunlight, in an idyllic setting. He has no prescience of the personal danger that awaits him.

The opening section has revealed that all the logic and tools of detecting will not help in the Blue Rose case. The murderer of Teresa Banks remains at large. A trained agent has disappeared. Another has moved through time and space to warn them of danger, but has failed because those who are watching do not want interruptions.

As Nochimson says: "The first thirty minutes of *Fire Walk with Me* tell us not to look to the logic of authorities to deliver us."[69]

---

[69] Nochimson, *The Passion of David Lynch*, Kindle edition, location 3176.

V

The theme music for *Twin Peaks* sweeps in, and the sight of the road into the town, and its sign, establishes the return to the familiar. 'ONE YEAR LATER' flashes on the screen.

Laura Palmer (Sheryl Lee) walks through leafy suburbia (too green for February) with a book in her arms, a dreamy expression on her face. This is the world of Mom and Pop and apple pie. She halts in front of the big Hayward house and calls for Donna, who hurries down the steps to her. Donna is played by actress Moira Kelly in the movie because Sherilyn Fen showed no interest in reprising her *Twin Peaks* role.[70] The two young women exude the ease and happiness of good friends.

The girls drift through the safe street, and are briefly heckled by boyfriends Mike Nelson (Gary Hershberger) and Bobby Briggs (Dana Ashbrook) in their open top black car. It cuts to inside the High School, as the girls go about their classes. James Hurley (James Marshall) interrupts them to speak to Laura privately, and Donna keeps watch at a discrete distance. Later, the two girls are friendly as they talk in between classes, and Laura indicates she needs to go to the bathroom.

As soon as she is separated from Donna her expression changes: the mask she wears around Donna, the confident, all-American sweetheart, slips. She enters the ladies room, which is lit as cool, blue-grey, and enters a stall.

Perched on the toilet she sniffs cocaine expertly, and a bell rings. The first alarm that something is not right in Laura's world. Plus, an association has been established with Teresa Banks, who was reputed to be sniffing cocaine also. A short establishing shot of the exterior of Twin Peaks High

---

[70] This identity switch supports the message that *FWWM* is not what has gone before. Characters are being revealed differently. It is a useful accident that Lynch embraces.

School is shown, and the bright red door. Throughout this entire section the storytelling has been efficient, and mostly wordless, and thrumming through it all the strong theme song that keeps the pace moving.

The next cut is to a clock showing it is 2.30 pm. James loiters in a back room, being his usual moody self. The music turns sexy, and a door opens: Laura enters wearing only a white towel. This must be somewhere near the Gym, and it's risky behaviour for two teens. If caught by a teacher or other students they would be in trouble. Laura is not what she seems.

This action is intercut with Bobby entering through the red door into the school, not caring about class schedules. He swaggers up to the school's large glass trophy cabinet. At its centre is Laura's iconic Homecoming Queen photo: where she is styled as the perfect dream girl.

The symbolism here is clear: her image is centre to the reputation of the High School, and by extension, the town. She is trapped in an idealised image, and caged with the other trophies to be admired. She is always on display, and an object to be won.

Bobby, the school jock, stares at her, proud to be dating the prettiest, best-known girl on campus. "Hey baby," he says, and kisses the glass case noisily.

This sweet girl image is subverted by the next shot of her and James together, mid-way in conversation. She wants to be kissed, but he wants to talk. It's a twist on the formulaic girl/boy dynamic: Laura wants to live in the moment and have sex, but James needs their relationship status updated.

"It does matter, we're in love," he informs her, in an angsty fashion.

She is much more worldly. "Quit trying to hold on so tight. I'm gone. Long gone. Like a turkey in the corn." Turkeys are the birds slaughtered and dressed up as the centrepiece for the traditional thanksgiving feast.

James makes a joke about her being too smart, and Laura's face crumbles, her lip trembling. The conversation, which could have sounded corny, is desperate due to Lee's charged performance.

"Gobble, gobble," she says, shivering. It is poignant under the humour. His protestations of love seem alternatively to irritate and arouse her. She wants to believe him, but indicates that this is a leap of faith that she cannot truly make—her experiences have taught her that men will say anything to entice her to have sex.[71] She wears half of the heart locket, dangling between her naked breasts, her tag of hope for true love—something she doesn't quite believe in.

Later, Laura and Donna leave school and Bobby aggressively asks where she's been. She is cruel and cold to him, her face washed out, as if she's come down from her coke high. Bobby grabs her arm angrily, demanding she tell him who she was with. His jealousy is not without foundation.

Laura's steel emerges: "Get lost Bobby," she tells him.

"Oh yeah, you'll be calling soon and maybe I won't be around," he threatens. Bobby is her drug supplier. Again, Lee's performance is first rate here: Laura's expression shifts from cruel to wheedling in moments. It's a disturbing, mercurial transformation because it demonstrates her ability to switch personality depending on the demands of her audience. It's a skill

---

[71] Jennifer Lynch's book, *The Secret Diary of Laura Palmer* (London: Penguin, 1992), is a tour-de-force description of the contradictory forces tearing the young woman apart. It depicts her fraught personal journey, complex sexual identity, numerous lovers, and extensive drug habit. Sheryl Lee read the book, and kept it with her throughout the filming of *FWWM*. It no doubt helped to inform her characterisation of Laura. Lynch himself probably did not read the book. In an interview Jennifer Lynch says, "Truth be told, I don't think my father ever read the diary—which is both totally expected and a little sad." Quoted in Dennis Lim, *David Lynch: The Man from Another Place*, Kindle edition, location 1791.

honed by many children who grow up in traumatic environments. It's a worrying indicator that Laura does not have an intact central identity: she is too busy holding up whatever fractured aspect of herself that others demand in any given situation.

Bobby wants her to be the faithful pretty blonde who has sex just with him and does as he asks. Above all, Laura knows the cost of all transactions, and what is required to maintain her access to drugs. Drugs are the only thing that keep her numbed to what is happening in her life.

"Come on Bobby", she coos. She flashes the high wattage smile from her photograph, and he melts. All the lessons she has been taught in life are once again confirmed: her power comes from her sexual appeal and her availability for sex.

While James and Bobby have different personalities, they are both easily placated when she shows them what they want to see: in these cases the damsel or the cheerleader. When she reverts to passive tactics that devolve power to them they are happiest. Any time she reveals her strength and complex nature to men they reject her.[72]

---

[72] Jennifer Lynch gives voice to this frustration in *The Secret Diary of Laura Palmer*: "I feel like a fake, I told him (Dr. Jacoby), even though I was Homecoming Queen, I had such a story behind my smile in the photos and at the football game as well. ... I told him it felt like the school and the town and the world were mocking me by voting me Homecoming Queen ... How could they not see how I was being swallowed up by pain?

Bobby, his masculine authority reasserted, puffs up and swaggers back to school. Laura, in full giggling, vacant mode, blows him a kiss.

In the next scene the girls lounge in the Hayward living room, on plush, comfortable chairs, in front of a roaring fire. The carpet is a soft pink. The scene is shot from above, and Laura is lying upside down in a chair while Donna lies flat on a sofa. Cinematographer Ron Garcia said in an interview the system of high and low angle shots were carefully devised: "The high-angled shots reflect an angelic presence that continues throughout the film, with an unseen angel looking down on the evil events below."[73]

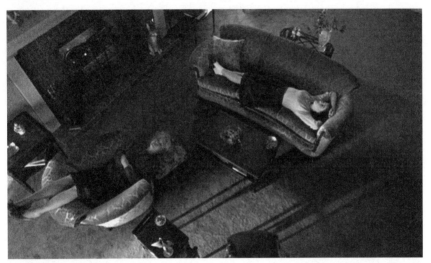

Laura is a person who increasingly believes she is doomed, but throughout the film Lynch subtly implies that there is a light watching over her that dilutes the pervading darkness into which she is plunging. That light is the strength of Laura's innate spirit that retains its purity despite the trials she endures.

She describes her fatalism in this scene, after Donna questions her plans for the evening. While she is more at ease with Donna than with many of her other companions, Laura has not yet revealed the full extent

---

How dare they make me a spectacle like that and ask me to smile again and again and again!" p 233.

[73] David Hughes, *The Complete Lynch* (London: Virgin, 2001), p 159.

of her night time activities to her friend. Laura is a person who creates discrete boundaries around her relationships to control the territories in which people operate, and mostly, to protect her fractured selves. This defence mechanism also means she has successfully hidden an important piece of information from herself to maintain her sanity: the 'true' identity of BOB.

Like many girlfriends, they discuss boys. Donna is dismissive when Laura mentions seeing Bobby (ironic coming from the girl dating the boorish Mike Nelson). The girls are looking up at the ceiling, not at each other, allowing them to be philosophical and truthful. Donna's face lights up when she discusses James. The camera cuts between both women. Donna has a virginal, romantic notion about love, and when the camera focuses on Laura's face in this exchange she is both cynical and suspicious of Donna's description of her secret boyfriend.

Donna switches subject, and hypothesises: "Do you think that if you were falling in space that you would slow down after a while or go faster and faster?" As the camera cuts between the two of them it presses relentlessly into a tight close-up of Laura's face, while Donna remains safely in a mid-shot.

Laura knows the answer to this, as she is experiencing it: "Faster and faster. For a long time you wouldn't feel anything. Then you're burst into fire. Forever. And the angels wouldn't help you. Because they've all gone away." A faint sound of the wind accompanies her monologue, and at the end Laura's powerlessness is transfixing—Donna says nothing.

The story moves, with Laura, to the Palmer house—large, white, with a wreath of a heart hanging from the centre of the door. Laura must ascend a wide set of red brick steps to get in.

She calls out to her mother, and scoots up to her bedroom, where she can be freer. She sways to a funky song[74] and smokes a cigarette as she retrieves her diary from behind the chest of drawers in her bedroom. She lies on her belly on the bed, tapping ash into her glass ashtray, and flicks through entries in the diary—until she comes to a section that is torn out.

There's a sound like tearing—not only is it like the echo of the act of vandalism and invasion of privacy, it's also a wounding rent in Laura's sense of personal safety and her psyche. Her hands shake as she examines the diary and finds another entry torn out. The ripping sound occurs again.

She runs into the hallway for the stairs, that transitory space, with the ceiling fan shadowed above.

She drives in a rush to Harold Smith's house—one of her secret people. Most of them are unaware of the others, but that's how she's remained safe so far, by keeping BOB from knowing everything. This intrusion has breached one of her many defences.

Harold, a shut-in who grows orchids, has retreated from the world completely, which is his way of avoiding hurt. Laura has penetrated his fortress because he is lonely, and as always, her attractiveness is the key to all doors guarded by men.

Harold's room is walled in by books, which are his only escape and companionship, other than the difficult flowers he cultivates. Yet, for all his knowledge, he is vulnerable to people. Repeatedly Lynch makes the point that instinct is as vital as facts. Laura confides that she believes that BOB has torn out pages of her secret diary, and Harold reveals that he doesn't believe that BOB is real. In this way he echoes Sheriff Truman's disbelief in *Twin Peaks* that Leland is also BOB.[75]

---

[74] 'A Real Indication', the first original song of the film, with lyrics by Lynch, and music/vocals by Badalamenti, could almost be a Tom Waits song.

[75] "I'm having a hard time believing," he states, despite witnessing Leland's possession by

"There are pages torn out, that is real Harold!" He inspects her diary, and Laura trembles with conviction. 'BOB is real. He's been having me since I was twelve.'[76]

This is the first explicit reference to the abuse that Laura has been enduring for the past five years, and she is incensed that someone might imply that she is not experiencing that terrifying ordeal. This is always the great fear of the victim of abuse, that they will not be believed.

As she continues to speak of BOB to Harold—probably the first person she has confided in about her abuse—she becomes increasingly agitated.[77]

"He says he wants to be in me or he'll kill me," she says.

Harold, appalled, backs away from this, but Laura presses forward, and grabs his shirt.

"FIRE. WALK. WITH. ME." she growls, her teeth bared.

There is a momentarily flash, where Laura 'becomes' something else. Her discussion of BOB, and the trauma she has experienced, combined

---

BOB. Cooper responds, "Harry is it easier to believe a man would rape and murder his own daughter? Any more comforting?" ('Arbitrary Law', *Twin Peaks*, season two.)

[76] In Jennifer Lynch's *The Secret Diary of Laura Palmer*, BOB is always capitalised, and at one point Laura notes that it makes its own warning: 'Beware. OF. BOB'. p 93.

[77] Laura had also been seeing the psychiatrist Dr. Lawrence Jacoby (Russ Tamblyn) for six months prior to her death, but it's not clear how forthcoming she was about all of her experiences.

with the summoning words, has invoked the possessing demon. Her face is painted white, her lips are black, and her teeth are white against red gums. It's almost as if she is going to take a bite out of Harold.

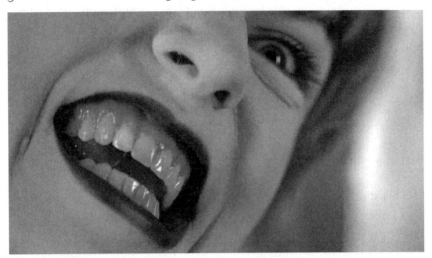

The temporary possession terrifies Laura and she snaps back to herself, crying on his shoulder. Harold is equally spooked. She gives him the diary, kisses him passionately, before running to the door. "I don't know when I will come back. Maybe never," she says. Laura is aware that the devouring presence of her tormentor is close and trying to discover all her secrets. Her retreat is her only way to secure this private part of her life.

The next scene shows the slowed down ceiling fan in the hallway of the Palmer house, it thrums. This is a signal that Leland is about to abuse Laura—Leland always turned the fan on to mask his visits to her daughter's room.

Shot from above, Laura is crouched on the floor, against a white wall and saturated with light. She's wearing a red shirt, a sign that she is edging closer to becoming a resident of the Red Room. BOB's voice hisses: "I want to taste through your mouth."

Her image dissolves to the red curtains of the Red Room. The discovery of her diary by Leland/BOB, and her conversation with Harold, has brought her to the precipice and caused a spiritual assault.

Laura has been trying to let people know about her abuse by acting out through drugs and being promiscuous, yet that behaviour was tolerated by the townspeople and those who wanted to exploit her. But once she speaks of her assailant she is attacked and silenced.

The red curtains dissolve to show Agent Cooper in Philadelphia, telling Agent Rosenfeld that he has a premonition that the killer will strike again, and Albert will help him solve the case. Albert tests Cooper's insight by asking him questions about the next victim.

Cooper, focused on some inner knowledge, says: "She's in High School. She's sexually active. She's using drugs. She's crying out for help."

Albert scoffs at this, noting "You're talking about half the High School girls in America!" When he presses Cooper to tell him what she's going in that moment he responds by saying "She's preparing a great abundance of food."

This short scene, partly played for humour, shows that Agent Cooper and Laura Palmer share an important, invisible connection. They are quantumly entangled, and while it might seem from *Twin Peaks* that Cooper will be the saviour, it is going to be Laura who saves him. It is she who has experienced the Red Room, its inhabitants, and their twisted agenda. She will pass through there first, and it is she who will guide him when he needs her most.

The story returns to Laura preparing her meals on wheels service at the beloved Double R Diner. This is one of Laura's 'good girl' jobs, part of her on-going performance as Laura the Homecoming Queen, and something she does to counteract the internal hatred she fosters because of her abuse and her night time activities. But the worlds that she has steadfastly kept separate are colliding, and soon everything will be chaos.

Norma Jennings (Peggy Lipton) encourages Shelly Johnson (Mädchen Amick) to help Laura because Heidi (Andrea Hays) has a bloody nose. It's not stated what caused the injury, but it could be a reaction to a reality breach happening outside the diner. The blood, and the colour red, are a signal for danger.

As Laura loads the station wagon, she looks up and see Mrs. Tremond and her grandson in the bright daylight. Her grandson is wearing his white mask, and carrying a stick just like the Jumping Man. Behind them are train tracks, and a white crossing sign that states 'RAILROAD

CROSSING' (it creates an 'X', a crossroads). In this way Mrs. Tremond and her grandson could be considered 'crossing spirits', entities that come through to susceptible individuals and push them along to being possessed or manipulated. They have travelled along a different track to get here.

This is outright invasion of Laura's reality, and there is a burst of the blue static, to indicate channels switching.

Mrs. Tremond beckons to Laura with her leather-gloved hand. Laura moves to them, wary.

The older lady holds up a framed photograph of a room with wooden floors and a dark floral wallpaper that is blackened in places, as if a fire has occurred in the room. A red door is open. "This would look nice on your wall," she says.

The boy adds, "The man behind the mask is looking for the book with the pages torn out. He is going toward the hiding place." The boy's voice is perfectly distinct, but he is subtitled — Mrs. Tremond is not. The camera moves to a close-up of where the eyes should be on the white mask. "He is under the fan now."

Laura knows what these people are talking about: BOB is aggressively hunting for her most private thoughts. He wants to know everything about her so he can possess her completely.

Laura runs to Shelly, and the camera shows the woman and the boy walking towards the railroad. It's not clear if Shelly can see them too.

Laura babbles that she cannot do the meals on wheels, and dashes off with the photograph in her hand.

The next image of the Palmer house is shot low, from an angle—electricity wires cut across the sky above, and appear to attach into the house itself. It is a metaphor for the spiritual pathways that the attacking entities travel upon.

The fan is whirring, and shot from a different viewpoint than usual: directly below. Laura is at home, searching for her spiritual terrorist. She is hunched, defensive, as she walks through her home. She looks like someone in a war zone. This is not a safe harbour for her. She creeps up the stairs, and the sound of the fan is a warning. Slowly she opens the door, and she sees BOB, searching behind her chest of drawers for her diary.

She screams, and BOB roars at her in response. There is a shot in his open mouth, as if he is attempting to devour her completely; it is reminiscent of the similar shot in the scene above the convenience store.

Laura bolts out of her house, desperate and crying. She hides under a nearby shrub, and sobs into the lawn.

She looks up and sees her father leaving the house. "Oh my god, oh my god!" she cries, horrified. "No, no, no, no, no," she moans, and buries her face in the grass.

Leland drives off in his large convertible, oblivious to his daughter's breakdown.

"It's not him," she repeats to herself as the camera drifts to the framed photograph that Laura has dropped in her distress. Laura's doorway to knowledge is open.

Distraught, Laura turns to Donna, and is comforted. Their conversation is not shown, instead the story moves to the twilight period as Laura returns home, now a dangerous place for her.

Leland questions her immediately as she comes in, and directs her to sit at the dinner table. He acts as if everything is all right, until he sees the half-heart locket she is wearing. The sign of a boyfriend, and of course, sexual relations. He stands and moves beside her, saying that she hasn't washed her hands before food. He looms over her and asks for her hands, so he can examine them.

He grabs both of them by the wrists. "These hands are filthy!" he says. He peers at her left ring finger[78], and says "Look, there's dirt way under this fingernail." His intense, odd behaviour scares Laura, who is holding onto the belief that her father could not also be BOB.

Sarah Palmer (Grace Zabriskie) enters the room and sees Leland tormenting Laura, and she tries to make him stop. But Leland seizes upon the half a heart necklace and asks "Is this from a lover?"

---

[78] It's the same fingernail on Teresa's hand under which a letter was inserted after her death. This will also happen to Laura after she is murdered.

Sarah, deeply uncomfortable (and on some level, probably aware of what Leland has been doing), tries to placate him.

Leland ignores her and pinches Laura's cheek in a parody of a cute gesture by a Dad. "Did Bobby give you this? Or is there someone new?"

Sarah tries to convince her husband to stop. "She doesn't like that", she says, upset.

"How do you know what she likes?" he asks.

Sarah screams at him to stop. Laura is on the verge of tears. Finally, Leland returns to his regular spot at the table as father. He orders Laura to wash her hands, and she leaves the room crying.

With all the extraordinary scenes of horror and weirdness in *FWWM* this scene at the Palmer family dinner table is one of the most uncomfortable and difficult to watch, because it is couched in the everyday power dynamics of an unstable household in which no one will speak the truth. There is no need for red curtains or demonic entities: the awful pain of a broken family is upsetting enough.

It cuts to Laura sitting in her bedroom, and the clock reads 10.35 pm. She appears to be doing homework, but is staring into space, processing what is happening to her.

In a nearby bedroom Sarah stares at her reflection in the mirror and the back of her husband as she smokes a cigarette. There is a close-up of Leland's intense, angry face, as he rocks slightly on the bed. Then his face clears, becomes mournful, and he sobs.

He enters Laura's bedroom. "I love you. I love you so much," he cries, and kisses her forehead. "Goodnight Princess," he says, and backs out of the room. It feels like a permanent goodbye.

Laura cries and looks up at the picture on her wall. It's a colourful but sentimental image of a group of children and an angel, assembled around a table. It depicts the idealised kindness she should experience at her own family dinner table, and serves as a stark contrast to what has just occurred. It reminds her that she left Mrs. Tremond's photograph on the lawn. She retrieves it and hangs it on her wall, opposite her bed, regarding it as she falls asleep.

The scene jumps so the view is inside the photograph, looking at the open door. It presses toward the doorway, as discordant strings play. Beyond it are red curtains. As the camera moves into the second room it's revealed as a near-replica of the first, but with red curtains covering a second arched entrance. Mrs. Tremond is in this room beside the red doorway. The wallpaper behind her is severely blackened. She's wearing a black dress with a low neckline, and gauzy sleeves. She's from another era, a gothic figure. She points to the open door, and the camera pushes through to the next room.

This room is heavily shadowed, and the wallpaper is ruined. Mrs. Tremond's grandson stands there in his suit, with the oddness of a child wearing the clothing of an adult. A wise innocent or an adult living backwards. He raises his hand and clicks his fingers (like the magic trick he performed in *Twin Peaks*), there's the sound of fire gouting, and flames illuminate the room and the boy.

The fire has been summoned, so the red curtains fade in, and the zig zag floor.

Laura is dreaming of being in the Red Room properly for the first time. Lynch has said that the Red Room is different for each person when they enter.[79] It also seems that the circumstances and the frame of mind of the entrant also influence what manifests.

This is not Cooper's Red Room, but Laura's. In it is a plinth with a base fashioned with gold shell scalloping, and a black marble top streaked with white. On it sits the Owl Cave Ring. The surface is so shiny the mirror image of the ring is reflected.

Cooper walks in and looks around inquisitively. He sees the Man From Another Place. They regard each other.

"Do you know who I am?" the Man from Another Place asks. Cooper shakes his head.

---

[79] Nochimson, *The Passion of David Lynch*, Kindle Edition, location 4577.

"I am the arm," he explains, "And I sound like this.' He makes a whooping sound and taps his hand to his lips repeatedly. Cooper does not understand.

The Man from Another Place picks up the ring and holds it up close to the camera, offering it to us/Laura.

It cuts to Cooper, who instinctively knows this is dangerous. He stares directly at the camera and says "Don't take the ring, Laura. Don't take the ring." His speech is not subtitled, because he is not a resident (for now) of this realm.

Laura wakes up in her bed with the warning still being spoken.

She holds her left arm as if it is numb. She stares around her room, and beside her in bed is Annie Blackburn[80], with a blood on her face.

She lifts her head and says, "My name is Annie. I've been with Dale and Laura. The good Dale is in the lodge and he can't leave. Write it in your diary." This is a warning from the future, possible because Laura is still asleep.

---

[80] Annie is Agent Cooper's girlfriend in *Twin Peaks*, and the sister of Norma Jennings, who owns the Double R Diner. She has left a convent (a place removed from the world) when she is first introduced, and is out of step with everyone else. In the final episode of *Twin Peaks* during the elaborate Red Room sequence, her identity is conflated with Cooper's previous, murdered, lover: Caroline Earle (Brenda E. Mathers). It's another of the dual identity/mirror selves that popular the series and the film.

Laura stares about again, and the music dials up. She opens her left hand, and she is holding the Owl Cave Ring. She gasps in horror. She closes her hand and the music stops.

Laura walks to her door, and opens it to check out the hallway, but there is no one there.

Relieved, she turns back into her room, and sees the new photograph on the wall. In it she is poised in the same action, turning in the doorway, looking at another room. She is on the threshold of knowledge, explicitly doubled: both identities available to herself.

The real Laura is stunned, staring at herself in the photograph—the double of Laura turns and stares at Laura in her bedroom—and there is a shift to 'reality' as Laura is back in her bed.

She wakes up and opens her hand—the ring is not there. It's daylight. She removes the photograph from the wall and places it face down on her table.

After a series of breaks with reality the film shifts focus to the more mundane world of drug deals and bad people. The truck driver/drug dealer Leo Johnson (Eric DaRe) is arguing with his wife Shelly about how to clean floors when Bobby phones him asking for more drugs using their coded language: "The football's empty. I'm looking for Santa Clause." Leo hangs up on him.

Bobby phones Jacques Renault (Walter Olkewicz), the barman at the Roadhouse, looking for drugs. "Two days, midnight. At the sound of sawing wood."

It cuts back to night-time at the Palmer house. Laura, dressed in a tight black dress, is having a scotch. Close by, her Homecoming Queen photo sits on a table in visible contrast. Donna arrives, wearing red lipstick and white ankle socks, a confused teenager playacting seductress.

Laura is in no mood to indulge Donna. She warned her friend previously that the night time is her time. The camaraderie that existed between them in the daylight has vanished. Laura is cold, and ready for action. She ignores her best friend, but Donna trails behind like a petulant child.

Laura arrives at the Bang Bang Bar—its windows are red, and it casts its light over her face. The Log Lady suddenly appears, stopping her.

She places her hand on Laura's forehead and says, "When this kind of fire starts it's very hard to put out. The tender boughs of innocence burn first, and the wind rises, and then all goodness is in jeopardy." She places her hand tenderly on Laura's face, and leaves.

Laura is stunned, her face bathed in the red light, and places her hand over her heart. She has been given a warning. Her end is coming if she doesn't swerve from her path.

She enters the bar where a singer (Julee Cruise), flooded in blue light, stands on a stage with a band, before red curtains. Cruise sings 'Questions in a World of Blue', another original composition by Lynch (lyrics) and Badalamenti (music).

Laura falls into a chair, deeply affected by the song. The singer is her voice of anguish—the voice that no one will listen to. Laura weeps, and when she notices Donna in the bar she cries harder. She pulls herself together, and lights a cigarette. Despite the warnings, and her intuition, she reverts to the role that traps her. She does not possess the maturity or experience to know how to change her course. She nods at Jaques, behind the bar, signalling her acquiesce to party.

Two men—Buck (Victor Rivers) and Tommy (Chris Pedersen)— spurred on by Jacques, arrive at her table. Buck lays down money in front of her.

"So you want to fuck the Homecoming Queen," she states crudely. It's

the blunt statement of Laura's understanding of her value: the gilded girl in the trophy cabinet. She is done with pretence.

"This ain't gonna get you a lot of loving," she tells him.

"You do go all the way, don't you little girl?"

She has had enough of patronising men. "Sooner or later," she replies. She rounds on Buck, reaches between his legs, and grabs him. "You willing to go all the way? Huh? You gonna do it to me?"

Her blunt statement of intent and aggression is a surprise and both men are rattled. They wanted pliant, not powerful.

Donna makes her move to the table. "Let's boogie," she says.

"What the hell are you doing?" Laura barks. Donna knocks back a shot and challenges Laura.

Laura kisses Buck, slipping back into the familiar mode of accommodating men's egos. Donna kisses his companion Tommy to indicate she's capable of making bad choices too.

"Okay Donna. Let's go."

The infamous 'Pink Room' scene begins: with moody red lighting, booze, cigarettes, a heavy guitar, and girls stripping, this is decadence incarnate, a hellish, human version of the Red Room. It's a combination of sexy with squeamish. Lynch designed the scene so that the actors were shouting, as one does in a club, and he always intended that the dialogue would be subtitled. He wanted to evoke the atmosphere of the clubhouse, yet ensure that the audience could understand the drug-addled conversation.

Being drunk at a club is a state of disconnected euphoria that's difficult to replicate successfully on the big screen, but through the alchemy of sound, lighting, and acting, Lynch recreates the unsteadiness and pleasure of being strung out and reckless. It's his unique magic trick.

Jacques is in situ, already wasted, and the foursome rock up to

him. Laura kisses him deeply, which only turns on her companions more. Donna pretends to be okay with everything, but she is uncomfortable.

They pass drinks around in a circle, and Buck slips a roofie into Donna's beer. It's unclear if Laura has noticed, and she encourages Donna to drink up. Here, Laura knows the score, and the drive for desire is not hidden. There is no inhibition or pretence. Or strained conversations.

On the dance floor Buck strips Laura's top off. She doesn't show any shame, and revels in her easy power over men. Initially shocked by Laura's behaviour, Donna begins to feel the effects of the drug and is disorientated. Laura doesn't notice because she's caught up in her own dream.

Laura sees Ronette Pulaski (Phoebe Augustine), who in *Twin Peaks* was either comatose or inarticulate. In the Pink Room some of her character comes through. She and Laura are old friends from One Eyed Jack's, and share a common background as exploited teenaged girls.

Donna spots Laura's jacket on the floor, and Tommy ties it around her waist. She embraces him enthusiastically and kisses him.

Jacques joins 'the party twins', Laura and Ronette, and Ronette mentions that Teresa Banks has been dead a year, and that she was going to get rich because she was blackmailing someone. Jacques reveals that Teresa wanted to know what their fathers looked like, which chills Laura. But the drugs and atmosphere distract her.

There's an extraordinary scene of a topless Laura getting head from Buck who is under the table while she slouches in a quasi-stupor beside Ronette. Laura feels in command in this room. Her desires are met and she believes she controls the men, but it is power lent to her, and it can be withdrawn on a whim.

She sees Donna, topless, bent over a table, being manhandled by Tommy. A bright white light hits Laura's face as epiphany and sudden sobriety seizes her. Her better self/angelic force has intervened at the last moment. Laura understands how close her friend is to having her life derailed.

She screams, and drags Jacques to help her. She pushes off Tommy, and gives out to Donna for wearing her top. This is not the actions of a peeved teen, but the fear of contagion. As if Donna may become more like Laura if she were to wear some of her clothing.[81]

Jacques picks Donna up bodily to remove her from danger. The final tracking shot of the room is of the filthy ash-ridden floor, littered with dozens of cigarette butts, and empty beer bottles. This is the crud that lies beneath the fun of the party.

---

[81] This is evident in *Twin Peaks* after Donna starts wearing Laura's sunglasses: she begins smoking cigarettes and being more seductive with James. It's more playacting, but it draws Leland/BOB's attention, and she narrowly avoids attack.

VII

In an atmospheric Lynchian segue the camera cuts to dark, mist-coated forests on a steep hillside, then it lightens to green trees in sunlight, and then the sight of the Hayward house in daylight. There is a sense of having emerged from the smog of the heavy night and the first inhale of a dewy morning.

Leland pulls up outside in his car. Inside, Donna and Laura sit on the couch. Laura appears completely recovered, but Donna's a mess, with no memory of how she got home or what happened at the club.

"I do love you Laura," Donna says.

Laura softens. "I love you too Donna. But I don't want you to be like me."

Donna asks the unanswerable question: "Why do you do it?"

Leland arrives, and ends their conversation. He sees the two girls embracing in friendship, and he has a flashback to the memory of Ronette and Laura, dressed in lingerie, on a motel bed.

Leland reminds Laura of their date with Sarah for breakfast, and the friends take leave of each other.

Leland drives Laura in his big convertible. There's the slight sound of the Man from Another Place yodelling, then a camper van chases after their car. Laura notices a smell like something's burning—the cue for a breach of time and space.

The van pulls around a traffic jam in a screech of tires and cloud of dust. Philip Gerard (Al Strobel), the One Armed Man, is behind the wheel. He is the host vessel for another supernatural entity 'MIKE', who is an adversary of BOB's.[82] Engines rev, music blares, and Leland honks the horn of his car attempting to ensure Laura does not hear what Gerard is shouting.

Gerard/MIKE is speaking to BOB who is inhabiting Leland at this point, and angry with BOB over a theft of their spiritual nourishment—the creamed corn that was shown in the bowls above the convenience store. It's a metaphor for the grief and pain they extract from the people they torment. When MIKE and BOB were hunting partners they used to cause a great deal of mischief, but MIKE had a road to Damascus moment, and severed his contact with BOB.[83]

Gerard yells, "The thread will be torn, Mr. Palmer, the thread will be torn."[84] And a Rottweiler barks.

Then Gerard waves the pinkie on his right hand—he's wearing the Owl Cave Ring. "It's him," he screams at Laura, "It's your father." But Leland is shouting to drown out the information, and Laura shrieks in fear and confusion.

The traffic unsnarls, and Leland makes his escape, skidding into 'Mo's

---

[82] It could be that MIKE is another name for the Man From Another Place. It's stated as much in the *FWWM* screenplay, and Cooper seems to make that association in the 'Arbitrary Laws' episode. All the spirits have their vessels: BOB has Leland, and the Giant has the Elderly Waiter. In a later scene in the film it seems likely that Gerard is the host for MIKE/the Man From Another Place.

[83] Gerard cut off his left arm because BOB and MIKE had the same tattoo while they were preying on humans. Which is quite extreme even for a bad break-up.

[84] Perhaps a reference to BOB's threat in the 'Arbitrary Laws' episode when he is about to kill Leland: "Leland is a babe in the woods with a large hole where his conscience used to be. And when I go children, I will pull that ripcord."

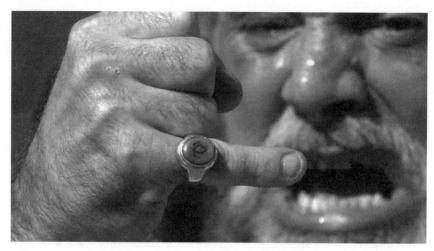

Motor' garage. Leland babbles and shouts at the garage attendants, and
Laura asks him if he's all right.

Leland's face stares at the camera as he is lost in another memory.

It's a page of *Fleshworld*—Teresa Banks, wearing a corset and her red
lipstick stares out of a grainy photograph. Leland notes that she looks "just
like my Laura."

A cut to a red neon sign for 'Motel' against a blush sunset sky. For the
first time Teresa is shown alive, even if it's in a flashback. She lies in bed

with Leland, staring off to one side, cigarette in hand, already setting up their next 'date'.

"The next time let's party with those girlfriends you told me about," Leland suggests.

She agrees, and suddenly he clamps his hand over her eyes, pushing her head down into the pillow. It's a display of power and control. "Who am I?" he asks.

Teresa remains calm. "I don't know," she replies.

Laura's shouting snaps Leland out of the memory. "Who was that? He looked familiar. Have I met him?" Her vague recognition of Gerard could be that he's hosting the entity MIKE, and Laura has much experience dealing with her father's possessing spirit BOB.

Leland covers up, acting confused. And it prompts another memory. Of him arriving at the motel to discover Ronette and Laura sitting on a bed together, talking and laughing. When he sees his daughter Leland is transfixed, then bolts. He gives Teresa cash, and runs off.

Teresa, smart cookie, begins to guess that one of the girls has a personal connection to Leland. This intuition will lead of her death.

As Teresa watches Leland leave, Mrs. Tremond's grandson jumps out from behind a building, wearing his mask, and holding the stick. He begins to caper about, like the Jumping Man, as the song, 'The Black Dog

Runs At Night', simmers underneath the scene. Again, it is like a discordant spell has been cast. Once the crossing spirit appears people are pushed along or destabilised.

There is the possibility that Mrs. Tremond's grandson was not in the original event, but has entered Leland's memory of the past. It is a type of dream space after all, where those entities exist and can easily traverse.

It could be that the grandson is stirring things up between BOB and MIKE.

The view returns to Leland in the car, and a change takes place. His memory of his daughter prostituting herself seems to have made up his mind.

Laura asks if Leland came home during the day last week. He denies it, until Laura presses him. Then he lies about needing aspirin. It's another terrific acting moment by Ray Wise who shows that Leland is just as adept as his daughter at shifting from one personality to another.

The evidence is piling up for Laura about the identity of BOB.

It follows with a close-up of Laura's clock at 8:00 PM, and a slowed memory of Gerard, waving the ring, and mouthing the words "It's him."

Laura sits dejectedly in her robe in her bedroom, considering her fate. She remembers the Man from Another Place holding up the Owl Cave Ring to her. She knows the man in the car was wearing the same ring. And she remembers: Teresa Banks in the Motel Room, wearing the same ring.

Her head jerks back so she looks up at the ceiling and her face is lit up with the bright light of insight. The camera cranes up to look down upon her. The light sizzles.

"Who are you? Who are you really?" She demands, but receives no answer.

Downstairs Leland paces, dwelling on the memory of his past crime. It cuts to the static on the TV screen from the opening shot in the film. Leland's expression is furious. Then the hammer crashes into the TV. Leland charges at Teresa who is huddled on a couch in a trailer. He viciously smashes her with the hammer, and again on the back of the head when she tumbles from the couch. Leland's face indicates he is not unhappy with that memory of brutality.

Upstairs, Laura inhales her last hit of cocaine from her little bag. The next day she meets Bobby in school, and he tells her they are going to get a big score of drugs.

That night, Laura, drunk and stoned, accompanies Bobby to the woods to make the drug connection that Jacques set up. Their only illumination is the single round torchlight in the dark forest. She is wasted, and giggling.

Deputy Cliff from Deer Meadow appears. He pulls out a huge bag, of what looks like cocaine.[85] Laura goes over to inspect it, and he yanks out his gun.

Bobby shoots him while Laura screams.

Laura repeats "Bobby, you killed Mike". She is traumatised and in shock, and laughs hysterically while Bobby ineffectively tries to bury the dead lawman. The assumption is that in her state Laura is referring to their friend Mike Nelson, but since the entity opposing BOB is called MIKE, there is room for speculation about the extent of Deputy Cliff's involvement with the entities out of time and space. Perhaps Deputy Cliff was a host for MIKE, and trying to eliminate Laura, the next host marked for BOB.

It cuts to the next day and James Hurley driving up to Laura's house on his motorbike, and pouting about a missed meeting. Leland watches disapprovingly above them, and Laura retreats to the house.

Later that night she does lines of coke. Leland gives his wife a drink of milk, which contains a sedative. Then he turns on the fan in the hallway.

---

[85] In a cut scene it is revealed that it is a bag of laxatives, not cocaine.

Sarah, dazed, looks up and sees a white horse in their bedroom, but she cannot say anything.[86]

In Laura's bedroom BOB climbs in the bedroom window and she acts aroused by him. He crawls over her, and begins to have sex with her.

She grabs his face and repeatedly asks, "Who are you?"

Laura screams when her mind finally breaks its seal of protection, and she allows herself to acknowledge that BOB is also her father.

---

[86] In *The Secret Diary of Laura Palmer* Laura used to own a white pony when she was a girl. It was a gift from Benjamin Horne (which she was led to believe was from her father), and might be the first instance where Laura is being groomed with gifts. Laura adored the pony, but eventually rejected it when she finally understood the complicated nature of the gift.

VIII

The following morning Leland acts like nothing is amiss. This is the old game that he used to play. Laura can't even look at him.

"Stay away from me," she hisses. Now that she knows, she will not allow it to happen again.

Leland's face transforms to a cruel expression.

Laura walks to school in blinding clear sunlight. The camera swings about to take in the electricity wires overhead, and the hiss of static is heard. She is operating in a state of shock. Her world has been shocked, and she no longer has any bearings.

In school, the hands of the clock spin on fast forward, blur, and overlap. Reality is pliable.

Later, Laura meets Bobby at his house. She doesn't want to have sex with him, but needs to score drugs. She is bereft, and even Bobby's heart is affected by her vulnerability.

Up in her bedroom Laura, dressed in lingerie, sniffs more lines of coke to deal with what she has planned for the night. It's a scene of amusing realism as she talks to James on the phone and attempts to put on a stocking with drunken slowness.

She notices her childish picture on her wall—the angel vanishes while she looks at it. From now on, Laura is in severe jeopardy. Even her angel has disappeared.

Laura sneaks out of her house, and rides off with James on his motor-bike, but Leland's demonic face glares out of the window. He has seen her absconding.

When James tries to discuss their relationship again, Laura accepts his kindness, then slaps his face to try to drive him away. He remains steadfast in his belief in their love.

She is obliterated, and wavering between states of mind. "He might try to kill you," she gasps, and then screams as if she has witnessed something terrible in the woods—last night's murder is only sinking in.

"You don't even know me. There are things about me. Even Donna doesn't know me. Your Laura disappeared." (As did her angel.) "It's just me now." And experience has taught her that most men don't want Laura the person, they want the trophy, or whatever fantasy they imagine her to be.

Even James fails in this situation. He tries to force a kiss on her and she becomes like stone. This is the worst tactic she has endured: a man bending her to his will.

"I think you want to take me home now," she says coldly.

A traffic light hangs from a wire in the darkness; the red stop light showing. It's a typical atmospheric intercut from *Twin Peaks*, but the first time it's been used in the film. James slows down, and Laura throws herself from the bike.[87]

"I love you James," she screams, and runs into the woods. She has no hope for herself any more. The performance by Lee of Laura's anguish and torment in these scenes with James is exceptional.

The light switches to green and James roars away on his bike.

---

[87] This is the intersection of Sparkwood and 21, which is mentioned several times in the TV show. In an excised scene from the film Dr Hayward tries to cheer Laura up by performing a magic trick: he attempts to pull a red rose from under a red cloth, but nothing manifests. He says, "You know the light at Sparkwood and 21? It worked right there. I just did it right there." In the screenplay it's also revealed as the location where Gerard/MIKE verbally assaults Leland and Laura in the car. It's a crossroads of strange power.

IX

Further in the woods Laura staggers up to Jacques; Leo is leaning against his red car, with Ronette. They've been waiting for her.

The music from the Pink Room scene starts up again, and in the cabin the girls prepare for their night of sex. Laura looks at herself in an oval hand mirror, and hands it to Ronette who fixes her scarlet red lipstick—the same shade as Teresa Banks.[88] The couples have sex while Waldo, the mynah bird, watches.

Laura's lipstick gets smeared over her mouth so she looks like a clown, or someone who is bleeding. They do more drugs and booze. Jacques ties Laura up as she protests, pleading with him to stop. Ronette tries to get up to help her but Leo stops her. The power Laura exerts over men can easily be overthrown when they wish to exert their dominance.

At the same moment Leland appears outside at the window, voyeuristically watching his daughter being restrained and raped. White light flashes as reality disrupts. The camera pulls back to the flames in the fireplace in the cabin. The fire has arrived.

Wind pushes through the trees, and Jacques staggers out of the cabin. Enraged, Leland beats him. Leo gets dressed and sways to the door, ignoring Laura's plea to be untied. Outside, he sees Jacques on the ground, and he runs away. Ronette is curled up in a ball on the bed.

When Leland enters the cabin Laura spots him and screams: he seizes her and screams in her face in response.

It cuts to an outside shot of the cabin as the cries ring out in the forest, and the One Armed Man runs toward the mayhem.

---

[88] One of the first moments in the pilot for *Twin Peaks* shows Josie Packard (Joan Chen) sitting before a mirror, checking her 'face'. Josie plays multiple parts for different people in the series. Both Laura and Ronette are prepping for their next performance.

Leland shoves his daughter and her friend out of the cabin. He has tied them with a rope leash and drives them before him like animals. Light from torches spins in their faces as they cry and Leland grins manically.

He takes them to the abandoned train carriage. From outside, a light bobs within as they are forced deep inside the broken space. Their shrieks tell their terror.

Inside Leland shines a light on them, striding around them in a circle, marvelling in his power over them. BOB and Leland are intercut as they torment the girls.

Leland loosens their ties, and Ronette is left kneeling to one side, as if praying for salvation.

Leland places a mirror in front of Laura's face (an awful parody of her earlier primping), and she sees BOB staring back at her. This is most terrifying of all. She is on the verge of becoming his next puppet.

Blue static interrupts the scene, and the Man from Another Place is in the Red Room, shouting.

Leland shows her pages from her diary. "I always thought you knew it was me," he says.

BOB appears and tells Laura that he wants her.

Ronette, crying, says "I'm sorry," and a bright white light saturates the room. Laura looks up, and so does Ronette.

An angel has appeared, hanging in the air above them. The bedlam mutes. It's a vacuum, a moment out of time. Ronette, her face streaked with lipstick and mascara, stares up at the angel in adoration.

When the noise and music returns, Ronette's ties have been severed.

Gerard bangs on the door asking to get in, and Ronette manages to shove the train carriage door open a little. Leland notices. He batters her, and throws her out of the carriage.

Gerard tosses the Owl Cave Ring into the carriage, where it is lit up by a spotlight, before Leland slams the door closed again.

Laura puts the ring on her left hand, which is lit up by a spotlight, while Leland screams "Don't make me do this." Laura has chosen the artefact of power offered by MIKE, and BOB must act if he wishes to thwart his nemesis.

Leland stabs his daughter to death.

The montage of images of Laura being killed are intercut with blue static and the Man From Another Place shouting in the Red Room, with a heavy choral music as if for a requiem.

Laura dies. Her mouth, upside down, bloodied and smeared with lipstick, is open, but voiceless, like Teresa Banks. Knowledge about Leland/BOB has killed them both. At the point where the women can speak out about abuse, they are silenced.

Leland confiscates her half-heart necklace, and prepares to wrap his daughter's body in plastic.

Outside, Gerard cold-heartedly steps over the body of Ronette, destroying any illusion that he is on the side of good. She doesn't rate his attention. Gerard follows the agenda of MIKE, and to him and BOB, humans are only fodder (despite MIKE's claim to be different).

The last images are from inside the cocoon of plastic in which Laura rests. The audience has its last identification with Laura, now dead, and during it Leland and BOB's faces are intercut.

Leland carries her body out of the carriage. He briefly checks on Ronette by prodding her with a foot, but she is unresponsive. Ronette, the working-class girl, is nothing to him.

Leland sets Laura's body afloat on the water, and there is a sense of full circle, as her body turning up dead has set the cycle of stories in motion.

Leland walks to Glastonbury Grove, and its circle of sycamore trees. With his blood spell in place, the path to the Black Lodge opens, and the red curtains appear.

Leland enters the Red Room. Inside Gerard and the Man From Another Place sit in matching chairs.

Leland stands before them. He falls and hovers almost parallel to the floor, and then hangs suspended in the air. He is a puppet, and BOB, his grinning master, materialises beside him.

The Man From Another Place stands and places his right hand on Gerard's left shoulder, above his missing arm. They speak in unison, because they are connected. The Man From Another Place is Gerard's missing limb.

"Bob, I want all my garmonbozia (pain and sorrow)," they say.

BOB reaches up to Leland's torso, where his daughter's blood covers his white shirt. In flick of his hand BOB removes the blood and splashes it onto the floor in front of his counterpart. White light illuminates the Man From Another Place's face, and the blood vanishes from the zig-zag floor.

There is a close up of the Man From Another Place tucking into a spoonful of creamed corn.

And the strangest intercut of many in this film: the monkey's face returns, and the name "Judy" is whispered.

This is followed by a cut to Laura's face, covered in plastic, and the moment of revelation in *Twin Peaks* as Sheriff Truman and Dr. Hayward discover she has been murdered.

The scene shifts, tracking across the zig-zag floor to red curtains, and Laura sits, dolled up like a movie star. She looks up at Dale Cooper, who stands with his arm on her left shoulder—a replica of Gerard and the Man From Another Place. Her expression is sad and regretful at first.

But a white light shines over her face, and the Angel appears in the Red Room.

Laura nods as if hearing something. She begins to laugh uproarishly as tears streak down her face. Life and death is both funny and tragic.

She is with Cooper in her version of the Red Room, and she has been given her instructions on how to save him. He gives no indication that he can see the angel. He only looks down at Laura in her chair. The angel is superimposed over the room, a soothing presence which protects her.

It fades to sky-blue with a beatific chorus singing, and Laura's face, smiling.

X

On a couple of occasions in *Twin Peaks* there is mention of a White Lodge, the mirror of the Black Lodge that is more commonly depicted in the series. In the episode 'Masked Ball' Deputy Hawk says:

My people believe that the White Lodge is a place where the spirits that rule man and nature reside. There is also a legend of a place called the Black Lodge. The shadow self of the White Lodge. Legend says that every spirit must pass through there on the way to perfection. There, you will meet your own shadow self. My people call it The Dweller on the Threshold. ... But it is said that if you confront the Black Lodge with imperfect courage, it will utterly annihilate your soul.

It's appears that Laura has gained entry to the White Lodge because unlike Cooper she has been continually tested by her shadow self (BOB) and has proved too resilient for him. She has come through the trial by fire and has been proven worthy. This appearance of the angel to both Laura and Ronette was not in the screenplay, and from all accounts was created in collaboration with Lynch and Lee on the set when they were in the final stages of shooting the film.

In *Twin Peaks* when Leland is dying he says, "They wanted her. They wanted Laura. But she was strong. She fought him. She wouldn't let him in." He claims to see his daughter in the light waiting for him—but in the final episode of *Twin Peaks* at least one tortured fragment of Leland lingers in the Black Lodge.

Despite the bittersweet ending, the film remains the tragedy of Laura Palmer. She was the icon of beauty that many of the residents sought to possess and corrupt. In *Twin Peaks* she is the guilt of a town that did nothing to intervene to help her. No one wanted to hear her pain. They desired her smile and her compliance with her symbolic role. And if it took drugs to keep her numbed to her problems, there were those who were happy to supply them to maintain control over her.

The TV series only dealt with these brutalised women through fragments: Laura, Teresa, and even Ronette, were plot points. In *FWWM* they are given a better tribute, and there is real mourning for Laura and Teresa's passing. While there is hope for these women, it is not easily accessed in a world that ignores their suffering. Salvation through death is not optimistic, even if it takes the edge off their murders. Ronette survives, but barely. Twin Peaks is a dangerous place for women.

The final scene cut from *FWWM*, called 'Epilogue', starts with 'SOME MONTHS LATER' over an image of Glastonbury Grove. The story has caught up to the end of *Twin Peaks* in season two. Agent Cooper is stuck in the Red Room, unable to escape. Annie Blackburn, in a shocked state, is in the Twin Peaks hospital, wearing the Owl Cave Ring. A nurse attends her, and Annie repeats the message she gave Laura in Laura's dream. The nurse sees the ring, removes it from Annie's left hand, and places it on her left ring finger.

Immediately she looks in a mirror to admire herself: repeating the first images of *Twin Peaks*. The Owl Cave Ring is out in the world, seeking new vulnerable people to wed to otherworldly entities, or offering passage to become a powerful realised person after a journey of trials. The destructive version of Agent Cooper is at large, but his better self is being advised and guarded by the woman who has endured the fire: Laura Palmer. She is his intuitive side, currently isolated, but waiting to re-emerge.

There are many other story fragments cut from *FWWM*, but they were the crowd-pleasing pieces with beloved characters from the TV series. When Lynch had to pare the running length to 135 minutes he had to jettison those storylines first, and they were probably what dedicated fans of the TV show wanted to see most of all. Those unfamiliar with the *Twin Peaks* universe were offered a difficult, convoluted narrative with a traumatised girl at its centre. It dealt with rape, incest, drug abuse, and duelling supernatural entities, and it did little to help the viewer to process it easily.

The film was badly received. At its première in Cannes in May 1992 it was jeered by the audience, and critical reaction was savage. David Baron of the *Time's Picayune* called Lynch a 'repellent director' and *Fire Walk With Me* 'a lurid monstrosity.' Tom Gliatto proclaimed *Fire Walk With Me* a 'nauseating bucket of slop'. Roger Ebert, who had always been antagonistic to Lynch's work, continued on form, and said it was 'meaningless [and] simpleminded'. Owen Gleiberman of *Entertainment Weekly* opted for, 'The movie is a true folly—almost nothing in it adds up,' and Jeff Shannon of *The Seattle Times* stated, 'The film is an incoherent travesty of loose and dead ends.'

Lynch, like any human being, found the rejection of his work painful (he said he felt like he was "made of broken glass" at his press conference at Cannes[89]), the only saving grace for him is that he is happy with the work, even if others at the time couldn't appreciate it. He has said:

The biggest protection is to feel that you did something that you like. That protects you a lot. It's when you don't like what you've done, and other people don't like it, then it's a double whammy. It's very bad. And then there's often something in the air that keeps people from actually seeing the work for what it is. There's something else that's maybe not real that they're reacting to more than the work. If some time goes by, they see the same thing again but now it's more worthwhile. That happens sometimes.

I feel bad that Fire Walk With Me *did no business and that a lot of the people hate the film. I really like the film. But it had a lot of baggage with it. It's as free and experimental as it could be within the dictates it had to follow.*[90]

Perhaps another reason for the antagonistic, negative reaction to the film is that it challenges the people who loved the TV show for its charm and kookiness, by reminding them of the genuine horror at its centre. It underlines that rape, incest, and two gruesome deaths were the inciting incidents for their entertainment. By giving Teresa and Laura personality and life the film disrupts the conventional narrative in which murdered women are quiescent and silent, and it is up to clever men to solve their deaths. Detectives in *FWWM* are wholly useless.

Intuition and emotional connection, as well as rational thinking, are required when trying to solve the mystery of life. As Cooper discovers, this

---

[89] Rodley, *Lynch on Lynch*, p. 189.

[90] Ibid., p. 190.

opens up the person and makes him/her vulnerable in unique ways.[91] Laura is better able to deal with these complexities than Cooper, but she is too young and susceptible to the realities of being under her father's dominating power to survive. Together, Laura and Cooper may be able to prevent others from being caught in the crossfire of malignant energies.

It was five years before Lynch made another feature film, and that was **Lost Highway** (1997). He stuck with his avant-garde roots, and kept making challenging, discomforting cinema that examines our fragmented selves and dislocated identities. He returned to straightforward narrative with the profound *The Straight Story* in 1999, proving he could do it 'straight', but it was a minor detour from his usual interest in unconventional stories. An attempt to return to television, resulted in him re-working the material for the provocative **Mulholland Drive** (2001). He was quick to embrace the Internet age and digital filmmaking, and began to release work online. He completed his longest, and most challenging film, **Inland Empire** in 2006.

During this period, and since, Lynch continued to work as an artist, a musician, a documentary film maker, and a voice actor. He never stops creating, he merely switches media. Above all, painting and creating art is his first abiding passion.

Twin Peaks was a pivotal moment in American television history, and marked a significant change in the kind of work broadcasters (and pay-for-view channels) thought would be accepted by their audiences. Over the years *FWWM* has seen a major re-assessment by cinephiles, and it's accepted now as an important cult film by a provocative film creator.

And after decades, 'It is happening again': a new season of *Twin Peaks* will début on Showtime on 21 May, 2017. David Lynch and Mark Frost have resumed their creative partnership, and this time retain creative control of the entire series (and thus all the blame if it's not successful).

The series was developed as one continuous script co-written by Lynch and Frost, entirely directed by Lynch, and divided up into individual

---

[91] Cooper's first love Caroline Earle is murdered in front of him, and he is betrayed and badly injured by his mentor in the FBI, Windom Earle. Despite this he continues to figure out puzzles by relying on a profound compassion and unconventional techniques. It might help him solve crimes, but it makes him a target for irrational hatred and usurping forces. Cooper has more to learn about navigating such complex waters.

episodes after it was shot (which was completed in April 2016). Much of the old cast are returning, although some died beforehand, and others after the filming.

It will be fascinating to see how much of *FWWM* figures in the new series, and how many of its thorny questions will be answered. No doubt, many more will be posed.

Humour, charming oddball antics, and quirky dialogue are guaranteed, but eccentricity and challenging narrative forms are likely (and welcome).

In this new golden age of television drama, it could be that Lynch and Frost will be able to bring forth their best realised vision of Twin Peaks, "a place both wonderful and strange."

Selected Bibliography

Bushman, David & Smith, Arthur, *Twin Peaks FAQ: All That's Left to Know About a Place Both Wonderful and Strange* (Milwaukee: Applause Theatre & Cinema Books, 2016).

Dukes, Brad, *Reflections: An Oral History of Twin Peaks* (Short/Tall Press, 2014).

Frost, Mark, *The Secret History of Twin Peaks* (London: Macmillan, 2016).

Frost, Scott "Diane..." *The Twin Peaks Tapes of Agent Cooper* (Simon & Schuster, 1990) Read by MacLachlan, Kyle.

Hughes, David, *The complete Lynch* (London: Virgin, 2001).

Josue, Thierry, *Masters of Cinema: David Lynch* (London: Phaidon Press, 2010).

Lim, Dennis, *David Lynch: The Man from Another Place* (Icons) (New Harvest, 2015).

Lynch, David, *Catching the Big Fish: Meditation, Consciousness, and Creativity* (New York: Penguin, 2006).

Lynch, David & Engels, Robert, *Twin Peaks: Fire Walk With Me, Teresa Banks and the Last Seven Days of Laura Palmer*. Shooting draft screenplay, 1991.

Lynch, Jennifer, *The Secret Diary of Laura Palmer* (London: Penguin, 1992).

Olson, Greg, *David Lynch: Beautiful Dark* (London: Scarecrow Press, 2008).

Nochimson, Martha P., 'Desire Under the Douglas Firs' Film Quarterly, Vol.46, No.2. Winter 1992/93

Nochimson, Martha P., *The Passion of David Lynch: Wild at Heart in Hollywood* (Austin: University of Texas Press, 2012) Kindle Edition.

Nochimson, Martha P., 'Don't call Twin Peaks a 'cult classic" Salon.com Monday, 13 October, 2014 http://www.salon.com/2014/10/13/dont_call_twin_peaks_a_cult_classic/

Rodley, Chris (ed.), *Lynch on Lynch* (London: Faber & Faber, 2005).

Sheen, Erica & Davidson, Annette (eds.), *The Cinema of David Lynch: American Dreams, Nightmare Visions* (London: Wallflower Press, 2004).

Studios, Brad D., "Exclusive Interview with Twin Peaks screenwriter and producer, Bob Engels!" on http://braddstudios.com

Thorne, John, *The Essential Wrapped In Plastic: Pathways to Twin Peaks* (John Thorne, 2016).

Todd, Antony, *Authorship and the films of David Lynch: aesthetic receptions in contemporary Hollywood* (London: I.B. Taurus, 2012).